Swimming Pool Maintenance Made Easy

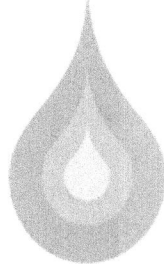

Second Edition

Revised 03/12/21

Written by: John Brace

MyPoolMadeEasy@gmail.com

Supporting information available at MyPoolMadeEasy.com

1

Swimming Pool Maintenance Made Easy

I've written this book to help make owning a swimming pool easy and question free. It is a step by step guide for pool maintenance. You will find a lot of helpful information about your weekly maintenance tasks and how the focus changes depending on the season. This book is meant to be a long term guide to help you maintain a beautiful, clean, clear, and healthy swimming pool and there are full explanations for each task performed and chemical used. I also explain each piece of pool equipment you own and talk about the energy efficient replacements available today. I hope you enjoy this book and refer back to it whenever you have questions about your pool maintenance.

Copyright © 2021 by John Brace
All rights reserved. This book or any portion thereof
may not be reproduced or used in any manner whatsoever
without the express written permission of the publisher
except for the use of brief quotations in a book review.

Swimming Pool Maintenance Made Easy

About the Author:

My name is John Brace. I have been in the swimming pool industry since 1995. That is also the year I graduated high school. I was the assistant manager of a swimming pool store during high school and later was the store manager of that store. I own a small swimming pool service and repair company in California. I started my business in 1999 and have serviced and repaired over 1,000 pools in that time! I am a licensed CA contractor and have

replaced hundreds if not thousands of pool pumps, motors, filters, heaters, pool cleaners, auto chlorinators, automated electronic controls, and so much more.

I am a very honest person and have always run my business that way. I never sell someone something they do not need! I feel it pays off in the end with their trust. I can't complain about my business, it is still thriving to this day. Even through the tough economy we have been having I don't have open spots for new customers on my route unless they are right next door to a current pool.

I wrote this book for a few reasons. The first is because I have heard too many times that after just a few minutes of explaining something to someone they have gained more understanding than

Swimming Pool Maintenance Made Easy

they had in ten years or more. I figure I should share my knowledge with more people that are confused and need my help. Also, I realized that I can only help a few people per year in just one location but I can help many more with a book. I would love to help you with your pool and make owning one easy and question free.

After reading this book you could start your own swimming pool service company if you wanted... or just be able to take care of yours with a lot less money and no more fear about the unknown. I hope you enjoy this book and refer back to it whenever you need it.

Swimming Pool Maintenance Made Easy

Contents

About the Author: 3

Introduction 15

Layout of This Book 17

Understanding Your Goals 18

Determine Your Pools Gallonage 20

The "Weekly Tasks" (All Seasons - Most Pools) 21

    Skim the top and bottom of the pool. 21

    Empty Skimmer basket(s) 22

    Empty the pump basket 22

    Empty the pool cleaner bag 24

    Test the pool water 25

    Look for algae or other issues 26

    Turn the pump back on and add needed chemicals 26

    Record your service 27

Summary of Weekly Tasks 28

Swimming Pool Maintenance Made Easy

Special Situations ....
28

Cold Climate (Freezing) Conditions ....
30

Spring Start-up and Maintenance ....
31

    If the water is clear and your pool was not winterized (covered) ....
31

    If you covered the pool for winter ....
32

    If the water is green or cloudy ....
33

Special Situations ....
35

    Vinyl Pools ....
35

    Freezing Conditions ....
36

Summer Season Maintenance ....
38

Fall Pool Maintenance ....
43

Winter Pool Maintenance ....
46

Special Situations ....
48

    Vinyl Pool ....
48

    Winterizing Your Pool - Warm Climates ....
49

Swimming Pool Maintenance Made Easy

- Step 1 50
- Step 2 50
- Step 3 51
- Step 4 51
- Step 5 52
- Step 6 52
  - Keep the Cover Clean and Dry 53
  - Check the Water Balance Once Per Month 53
  - Remove the Cover Early.. 54
- Winterizing Pool - Freezing Conditions 55

Getting down to basics 58

Testing the Pool Water... 58
- The Easy Part 58
- What type of test kit to use.. 59
- Ideal Ranges 60

Swimming Pool Maintenance Made Easy

Testing the Chlorine ....
60

Testing the pH ....
61

Testing Alkalinity ....
62

Testing Calcium ....
62

Testing Cyanuric Acid (Conditioner)..
63

Testing Phosphate Levels ....
64

Testing Total Dissolved Solids ....
65

Everything You are Testing and Why ....
66

How to Adjust your Chemical Levels ....
70

    Test Weekly ....
70

    Test Two Times Per Year ....
70

    Ideal Ranges ....
71

Adding Chlorine ....
72

    Types of Chlorine ....
73

    How much chlorine to add? ....
76

Swimming Pool Maintenance Made Easy

How long will the chlorine last? 78

Shocking the pool 79

How to adjust your pH and Alkalinity 80

How to Add Acid 82

Special Situations 84

Vinyl Liner or Fiberglass Pools - Raising pH 84

Adding Conditioner 85

Adding Calcium Hardness 88

Removing Phosphates 89

Killing Algae 91

Identify the type of algae 91

Killing Green Algae 91

Killing Mustard Algae 93

Killing Black Algae 94

Alternative Algaecides 95

Swimming Pool Maintenance Made Easy

Cleaning Your Filter ....
98
   Cleaning a Cartridge Filter ....
98
      Pent-air, Hayward, Waterway, or Jandy (4 cartridge filters) ....
98
      Sta Rite Cartridge Filter (System 3) ....
101
      Single Cartridge Filters ....
101
   Cleaning a Diatomaceous Earth (D.E) Filter ....
102
      Backwashing a D.E. Filter ....
105
   Backwashing a Sand Filter ....
107
Owning a "Salt Pool" ....
110
   Cleaning the "Salt Cell" ....
112
Ozonator and their Maintenance ....
114
Using a Flow Meter ....
116
Stain Prevention (Sequestering Agent) ....
119
   Calcium Buildup ....
119
Stain Removal ....
120

Swimming Pool Maintenance Made Easy

Ascorbic Acid 120

Oxalic Acid 121

   My Favorite Stain Removal Product (Company) 122

Alternative Stain Removal 122

New Pool Startup or Drain & Refill 124

   Step 1 - Sequestering Agent 124

   Step 2 - pH and Alkalinity 125

   Step 3 - Calcium Hardness 125

   Step 4 - Cyanuric Acid (Conditioner) 126

   Step 5 - Chlorine 126

   Step 6 - Re-test Everything 127

Re-Surfacing the Pool 129

Painting your Pool 133

Empty pool precautions 134

Choosing the Right Pool Equipment 137

Swimming Pool Maintenance Made Easy

Pool Filter 137

Pool Pump 139

   Single Speed Pump 140

   Two Speed Pumps 144

   Variable Speed Pumps 145

Pool Heater 147

Caretaker System (Pop Up Jets) 149

Robotic Pool Cleaners 149

In-Ground Pre Filter 151

Pool Has a Leak! 152

   The Bucket Test 152

   Leak Detection Companies 153

   A Long Term Leak Can Cause Permanent Problems 154

Pump Lost its Prime - What Now 155

Leaks at the Pool Equipment 159

Swimming Pool Maintenance Made Easy

Shade Cover for Pool Equipment 162

Lifted Concrete Around Pool 164

Settling Concrete 165

Coping Replacement 166

Tile Cleaning and Maintenance 168

    Loose or Missing Tile 169

Removing Rain Water from Pool 172

Plaster Problems 174

    Calcium Nodules and their Removal 174

    Blotching or Modeling Plaster and its Cause 176

    Staining, Streaking, or Fading Plaster 177

    Rust Stains on Plaster 178

    Pop Offs and Thin Plaster 179

    Tabs in the Skimmer 179

    Throwing Tabs at the Bottom of the Pool 180

Swimming Pool Maintenance Made Easy

Ducks in My Pool - What you should know 182

How Long Should I Run My Pumps? 185

    Booster Pumps 188

Main Drain Covers 190

Safety Signs, Equipment, and Rules 192

Pool Lights – Differences 197

    Changing out a light 198

Safety Covers 202

Solar Covers 204

Solar Panels on Your House 205

    Warm Water Conditions 208

Summary 210

Glossary with Lots of Extra Information: 212

Swimming Pool Maintenance Made Easy

Introduction

Thank you for purchasing Pool Maintenance Made Easy. **My goal is to make owning and maintaining your pool as easy as possible without causing additional problems that will cost you time and money.** Because of that goal I will try to teach with simple tasks and easy to understand language. I have taken a lot of time separating this book out into many different sections for easy reference and understanding. **Each section will explain a different part of pool maintenance and when you are done with the book you should have a good understanding of pool maintenance as a whole.** You can always refer back to any section later for a refresher.

I really do want to help you take great care of your pool so if there is anything you ever need extra help with that I did not cover in this book please do not hesitate to contact me directly at MyPoolMadeEasy@gmail.com or 916-224-7946.

I know that owning a swimming pool can feel overwhelming and that you might be afraid to make a costly mistake that might also waste a precious part of your swim season. The truth is, pool maintenance is not difficult at all if you have a good understanding of the tasks that need to be performed and why. After you learn how to take care of you pool equipment and the chemical balance you will have no problem maintaining your pool on your own. The biggest lesson you will learn is that **weekly maintenance is the key**. You should download and print the weekly maintenance log on my website and use it every week. I

Swimming Pool Maintenance Made Easy

will also be adding videos and blogposts to address topics not covered in this book and product reviews of new pool equipment over the years.

This book was written for all types of swimming pools and different climates that you may live in. There is however a difference for above ground pools versus any built in pool. There is also a big difference (especially in the off season) for any pool maintained throughout the Sunbelt states versus colder climates. I will be focusing on the more standard climates and on in ground pools throughout this book. I will however add extra information that I feel is needed for any other situation after each section. This extra information will be under the heading of "Special Situations". My goal is that anyone will find this book helpful no matter what type of pool you own or where it is located.

Swimming Pool Maintenance Made Easy

Layout of This Book

After a little bit of general information I have divided this book into 4 major sections (Spring, Summer, Fall, and Winter) for a few reasons.

The first is because it is easier to understand each season separately instead of grouping all things together. There will be some redundancy because of this.

The second reason is that I wanted you to be able to skip around and get more time-of-year specific information quickly when you are looking for it. **With that said, I still think that if you are serious about learning how to maintain your pool completely and gaining a holistic view of your pool, I would really encourage you to read the book from start to finish at least once.**

Lastly, I wanted you to feel less overwhelmed. As I have said before, owning and maintaining a swimming pool can be easy and trouble free most of the time. The problem is that every now and again, problems do arise. My goal in writing this book in this format is to cover the most pressing issues in each season without over complicating things. Throughout the rest of the book I try to address all of the other issues related to swimming pools separately. There is an index that should help to point you in the right direction when specific help is needed. If you cannot find the answer you are looking for in my book, feel free to email me.

Swimming Pool Maintenance Made Easy

Understanding Your Goals

Before we jump into "Spring", I feel it is best to take a second to explain to you what goals you should make throughout the year that will get you the results that you are looking for.

- The first goal would be to **keep as much debris out of the pool as possible**. That means leaves and dirt mostly. I suggest that you try to keep the yard as clean as possible around the pool in an attempt to have less enter the pool when the wind blows. This will make your life a lot easier in the long run because all of that dirt and debris draw on the chlorine and add unwanted phosphates to the water. I will explain chlorine demand and phosphates in more detail later in this book. For now just know that it is best to keep your pool as clean as possible.

- Your second goal should be to **set one day per week** as the day you maintain your pool and to keep a log of your weekly services. This is probably the simplest and most important piece of advice that I can give you and will yield a huge positive difference, especially if you have not been consistent in the past. It will make it easier later when all the times you have spent on your pool start to run together in your mind and you may skip a week and cause algae or cloudy water. **Please use the "Pool Maintenance Log" provided at the website for this**

Swimming Pool Maintenance Made Easy

book. You can write down the date and what was done every week to make things simple. At first it may seem like it is not needed and maybe even a waste of time but I assure you, once you get used to logging your maintenance, you will see why I recommend it. If you keep last years log you can even look back to compare things. I have a separate log for every pool that I am paid to maintain, I also keep a log for my own pool at home.

- The last goal you might set for yourself is to be **very diligent with how often you clean the pool filter**. The pool filter is responsible for the removal of all small particles in the water that cause cloudiness and eventually algae. It also keeps the pool water healthy because you cannot have bacteria in the pool unless algae are present too. If the filter is dirty and the pressure is high on the gauge, very little water is making its way through the filter and particles are being left behind to cause problems. **Think of these particles as food for algae**. I always explain, water that has a lot of small organic particles in it is like water with fertilizer in it. With just a little sunlight you will most likely have an algae problem. When you keep the filter clean the water flows smoothly through and the filter can continue to remove these small particles from the water. Just a side note on this topic, you may think your water has no particles in it because during the day the water looks clean. Turn on the pool light at night and look in front of it. If you see a lot of white dots in the water, where the light is, you have particles that the filter has not removed. This is why we need to run the pool pump enough time per day to accomplish one turnover. If your pool is 20,000 gallons, that is the number of gallons you want your pump to move each day. Calculating how

Swimming Pool Maintenance Made Easy

much water your pump is moving per hour is important. More on that later.

Determine Your Pools Gallonage

First things first, let's find out how big your pool is. Or more specifically, how many gallons of water it holds.

You will need to know the gallons in your pool for every chemical you need to add to the water. It is easy to figure out with a calculator. The most accurate formula for the standard in-ground pool is Length x Width x Average Depth x 7.5 = Pool Gallons. Most pools are not rectangles so you may need to change this formula to: Average Length x Average Width x Average Depth x 7.5 = Pool Gallonage.

Example: If your pool is about 32' long, 16' wide, 7' in the deep end, and 3' in the shallow end (average depth would be 5'). Your pool would hold about 19,200 gallons. You can either use 19,000 gallons or 20,000 gallons when you add chemicals.

If you have an oval or round above ground pool use 5.9 instead of 7.5.

In case you are wondering, or are sort of nerdy like me, there are 7.48 gallons of water in each cubic foot.

Swimming Pool Maintenance Made Easy

The "Weekly Tasks" (All Seasons - Most Pools)

Here is a quick overview of tasks that should be performed weekly all year long. All tasks will be talked about in more detail throughout the book. Some pools are winterized for the winter so those pools will only need these tasks performed during the time they are open. More on winterizing later in the book.

Perform these tasks once per week. Remember to keep a log of your weekly maintenance including the test readings and chemicals that you have added.

Skim the top and bottom of the pool.

Keeping the pool free of debris is just something you have to do. It is necessary because the debris will decompose and clog the

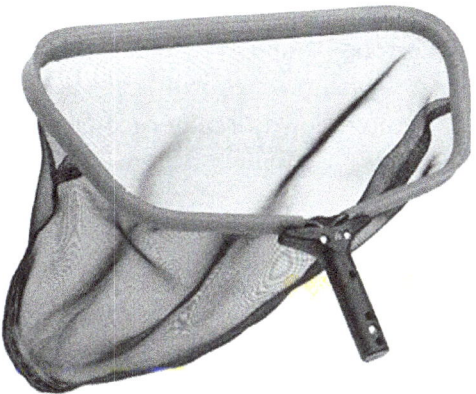

Swimming Pool Maintenance Made Easy

baskets and bags. It will also provide nutrition to many types of algae. All of which makes your job more difficult in the end. Most people only need to spend 10 minutes skimming the pool per week. **My suggestion is to get a great net and good pole**. They will cut the time and effort by half. They will also last two or three times as long as the cheap versions. I have a list of my preferred pool equipment at MyPoolMadeEasy.com.

Empty Skimmer basket(s)

Start with the skimmer baskets in the ground. It helps if the main pump is on because it keeps the leaves in the basket when you pull it out. Dump the leaves into a small bucket. Most baskets need a medium size rock as a weight. Be careful not to throw away the rock. Look at the bottom of the skimmer before you put the basket back to see if debris got past it. Clean any debris from the bottom of the skimmer. There might be a plastic flow regulator under the basket that will pull out to properly clean the skimmer. After the basket and skimmer are clean, put back the regulator and basket. Just a side note, there are baskets that have a weight and strong handle. These baskets are so strong they will likely be the only ones you will ever buy and they never need a rock to hold them down. I really recommend these baskets. More info at MyPoolMadeEasy.com

Empty the pump basket

Some of the debris that went around the skimmer basket that you just emptied will end up here in your pump basket. Also any

Swimming Pool Maintenance Made Easy

debris that was pulled from the bottom of your pool will be here. Pump baskets are usually smaller and need to be emptied every time there is debris in it.

Shut off the pump and clean the pump basket. Most pumps have a clear lid that unscrews or twists slightly counter clockwise to unlock. You can keep a rubber mallet next to the pump to use on the tabs of the lid if you like. There are also pump lid removal tools for the older style lids that screw onto the pump. Inside you will find the pump basket that simply gets cleaned out. Be careful not to drop the O-ring from the lid and not put it back. This is the number one way people damage the pool pump. Without that O-ring, the pump will run with no water going

Swimming Pool Maintenance Made Easy

through it (run dry). That will cause damage to the seals in the pump as well as the bearings in the motor. You should also try to keep the o-ring clean as well as the grove that the o-ring sits in so that the pump lid will seal properly and not let air in as the pump runs.

Empty the pool cleaner bag
With the pump off, carefully pull the pool cleaner out of the water and remove the bag from the top. Most pool cleaner bags have Velcro or a zipper on the bag to use when cleaning. **Not all pool cleaners have a bag to clean**. Some just have a hose and all debris goes to the pump or a small leaf canister in the hose (a clear plastic canister with a basket inside). If there is a leaf canister you will need to empty that when it is full by removing it from the hose and unscrewing the lid to take the basket out. You can clean the basket or bag weekly by just dumping the bulk of debris out and not caring about some of the small material still

Swimming Pool Maintenance Made Easy

left over or you can use a garden hose and thoroughly clean the bag or basket.

A side note, if you have a cleaner with a bag and you start to notice algae around the sewn parts, you probably have algae starting in the pool and you might think about using the 60% algaecide described later in this book to remove and prevent a bigger algae bloom. You can also soak the bag in a bucket of water with a small amount of bleach or liquid chlorine to remove the algae. The algae will come back to the bag unless you deal with the algae that is starting in your pool. The pool cleaner bags are often your very first indication that algae has started in your pool.

Test the pool water

Test the water for free chlorine, alkalinity, and pH weekly.

- Keep chlorine levels balanced between 1-5 ppm (Depending on season)

- Keep the pH maintained between 7.4 -7.6

- Maintain Alkalinity between 80 -120 (Gunite/Plaster/Pebble Tech pools) and 100 -140 (Vinyl or Fiberglass pools)

I will go into more detail about this later. It helps to write down the results on the log provided with this book (at website). After a few weeks you will start to get a feel for your pool. After a year you will know your pool and how it behaves each season. This will save you both time and money because you can prepare for what your pool needs before the next time you are at the store.

Swimming Pool Maintenance Made Easy

Look for algae or other issues

This is probably the most important part! **So many problems can be avoided if you notice small things happening before they become big things. Walk around the pool and look in all corners and crevasses. Look straight down the walls during the spring and summer to see if you notice any yellow.** It is a good idea to run **the brush down a couple of walls to find any hiding algae.** If you find any, brush all the walls and follow the algae removal steps in this book.

Turn the pump back on and add needed chemicals

Locate the air bleed valve at the top of the pool filter and open it. Turn the pump back on. The pool pump will need to "Prime" itself. This means that at first you will see your pump running with little or no water entering the pump basket area. After about 30 seconds you should start to see water coming into the pump. In another minute the pump housing should be full of water and if you have a variable speed pump it will automatically lower its RPM from its priming speed to the normal running speed. Air will come out of the bleed valve on top of your filter at first and then water after the pump primes. Shut the bleed valve when water comes out.

Follow the charts provided to determine the amount and type of chemicals that may be needed. Add the chemicals slowly while walking around the pool with the pump running. Always allow at least two hours after the last chemical is added before the pump turns off. This will ensure even distribution of any chemical.

Swimming Pool Maintenance Made Easy

Record your service

Use the service record paper at <u>MyPoolMadeEasy.com</u> on a clipboard or in a binder near your pool equipment to keep track of your weekly maintenance and all chemicals added.

Swimming Pool Maintenance Made Easy

Summary of Weekly Tasks

That was a simple set of instructions for what you should get used to doing every week regardless of the season. During the winter, after fall, you will not have a very demanding pool for a few months. **I urge you not to let the pool sit, or neglect the weekly schedule, and then perform a clean-up in the spring.** This is because it will probably cost you more money that way and it will certainly cost you more time. Not only time cleaning everything up but precious time that your pool will not be usable due to the way it looks and the high levels of chlorine and algaecide needed to rescue your pool. You just might lose half of your swim season due to bad planning. I have seen this way too many times to not mention it in this book.

Skim the pool and empty the baskets and bags all year long. It makes all the difference between a clean and easy to maintain pool and a dirty and impossible to maintain pool.

Special Situations

Above ground and in ground vinyl liner pools need a few extra notes at this point.

Most above ground pools do not have an automatic pool cleaner to help remove dirt and leaves from the bottom of the pool. You can buy a cleaner designed for above ground pools and they work well if the pump and filter you are using are large enough. You

Swimming Pool Maintenance Made Easy

would need to have a pump with a minimum horsepower of 1/2 and a cartridge filter no smaller than 100 square foot for a cleaner to work well. It is also possible you have a sand or D.E. filter. A sand filter would need to be a minimum of 1 cubic foot and a D.E. filter should be at least 24 square feet. If you do not have equipment this size or larger you can still clean the bottom of the pool with a manual vacuum and leaf net.

Vinyl swimming pools can be easily torn with a plastic net that is not in good condition. Always inspect your pool equipment and use them carefully so you do not cause damage to your vinyl liner.

Adding liquid chlorine or other chemicals to a vinyl liner pool require extra caution. You will need to make sure that you do not add liquid chlorine too close to the walls of the pool to avoid bleaching of the liner. Always run the pool filter when adding any chemical to a vinyl liner pool. Only use a nylon bristle brush on a vinyl liner pool. Never use a stainless steel brush or a vacuum with wheels. Equipment is made specifically for vinyl liner pools.

Above ground pools often have their pool pump and filter on the ground which is below the water level of the pool. This means that whenever you remove the pump lid or filter top water is likely to overflow from the pool unless you have ball valves or gate valves installed before the pump and after the filter. You will need to close those valves before you clean the pump or filter and open the valves again after the lids are back on before you turn the pump on. Failure to open those valves can damage the pump, pool plumbing, or the filter due to excess pressure.

Cold Climate (Freezing) Conditions

Swimming pools that are located in areas that freeze will not be kept open during the winter. After the pool is properly winterized most of the maintenance will be done to the cover itself and very little to the pool directly. Of course you should monitor your pool and the cover to make sure that no problems have started to develop, especially after a storm or extreme cold spell. Look for tears or separations in the cover and temporarily repair the cover to get through the winter. Repair kits or strong waterproof tape available at a hardware store or your local pool store might get you through the winter. Replace the cover before the next winter. I will talk about winterizing a pool in freezing climates later in this book. In warmer climates where freezing conditions are rare, I do not recommend covering swimming pools. It is usually more work to maintain the cover than the pool itself. Most pool pumps (variable speed) have a freeze system and they will automatically turn on and run all night long in a low speed to avoid frozen pipes. The low speed they run in costs very little in electricity. This will not be enough to avoid freezing in extreme weather.

Swimming Pool Maintenance Made Easy

Spring Start-up and Maintenance

If the water is clear and your pool was not winterized (covered)

Spring season starts around March or April. **There are several things that you can do now to make your pool easier to maintain during the summer season.**

Perform "Weekly Tasks" above and...

- Clean the pool filter (directions below)

- Balance the Calcium and Conditioner levels (see below)

- Clean the salt cell if you have one. See "cleaning the salt cell" for more info

- Add a preventative algaecide (algaecide 60) now before you see any algae (maintenance dose)

- Increase the run time of the pool filter to insure at least one turnover of your entire gallonage per day (usually 4-8 hours per day depending on equipment and size of pool)

- Start using tablet chlorine in a floater (1 per week per 20,000 gallons) or chlorinator at equipment pad

- Keep chlorine levels higher (between 3-5 ppm.)

- Keep the pH maintained between 7.4 -7.6

Swimming Pool Maintenance Made Easy

- Maintain Alkalinity between 80 -120 (Gunite/Plaster/Pebble Tech pools) and 100 -140 (Vinyl or Fiberglass pools)

Performing these tasks now before the summer will give you a huge advantage all summer long. The filter will be able to remove particles from the water that would be needed for algae formation. **With the water balanced and the preventative algaecide added, you should have a great start to a long swim season.**

If you covered the pool for winter

If you covered your pool for the winter, it is time to remove it now. If there is water on top of the cover you should use your sump pump to remove as much as possible. Try to clean any leafs

and dirt by hosing it to one corner and using the skimming net and pump again before removing the water bags or weights

Swimming Pool Maintenance Made Easy

around the perimeter. Drain the water bags and remove them from three sides of the cover. Fold the cover over the last side of the pool with water bags still on top of the cover. It is helpful if you have a second person for this. Try to fold the cover into 4' to 5' sections. When you get to the last part you can pull the cover out from under the last water bags. Take the cover to an open area and fold it the other direction until it is small enough to store. You can also open the cover up and thoroughly clean the cover and let it dry before storage if you have the space. Much of the folding options will depend you your pool and the available space around your pool. The idea is to clean and dry the cover as much as possible before storing the cover until next winter.

If the water is green or cloudy

Cloudy water is usually a pretty easy situation to overcome. Most of the time you will need to clean the pool filter, run the pump extra hours (10 -12 hours per day), balance the pool chemistry,

33

Swimming Pool Maintenance Made Easy

and raise chlorine levels to 5 ppm and maintain it there until the pool is clear. Sometimes the water will not clear or it is already green. You need to first think about how long the pool has been green or cloudy (not maintained) because the longer that was the case, the more difficult the pool will be to clear. I have found after all my years clearing green pools that if I make one big attempt to clear the pool and there are no noticeable differences in the water after a few days, I make the decision to drain the pool and start over. The water itself costs an average of $40-$60 and the startup chemicals would be about $80 for a 20,000 gallon pool. Compare this to a chemical cost of the same or more, plus the countless hours vacuuming and cleaning the filters, plus adding algaecides and gallons of chlorine. I have made the mistake of continuing the cleanup process long after I should have given up, more than once. In the end I only cost my customer valuable time and myself all of the money for the job on chemicals.

The one big attempt to clear the pool first goes like this: For a in-ground plaster pool you would first remove as many leafs from the bottom of the pool as possible. Second, clean the pool filter and all baskets and bags. Then, assuming there is no chlorine in the pool; add up to two gallons of chlorine per 10,000 gallons of pool water with the pump on. Immediately add one quart of algaecide 60 per 20,000 gallons of pool water. Run the pool pump for at least 12 hours. If the water looks a lot better the next step would be to continue to clean the pool (brushing and skimming) and to keep the filter clean (clean the filter whenever the

Swimming Pool Maintenance Made Easy

pressure goes up 8-10 lbs. over the starting pressure). The water condition will get better every day. You will need to add 2 gallons of chlorine per 10,000 gallons of water every time the chlorine goes to zero until the water is mostly clear. A second dose of algaecide may also be needed. Note: Chlorine added at this rate is extreme and considered a "super shock". Vinyl liner pools and plastic pool cleaner hoses are not meant to be in this much chlorine. Pool cleaners should be removed during super shock treatment and a lower dose of chlorine should be used to remove algae in vinyl liner pools. One gallon per 10,000 gallons of pool water would be about the max for sensitive pool surfaces.

If the water does not look better after this attempt, ensure all the chlorine is gone with your test kit, find the sewer clean-out for your house and pump the pool water into the sewer clean-out with a submersible pump and a discharge hose. You can rent this equipment or pay a pool company to do this for you. Safety information and cleaning tips can be found in the section called "Empty pool precautions and preparation".

Special Situations

Vinyl Pools

As mentioned above, above ground or in ground vinyl pools do not need extra information in this section with the exception shocking them to remove algae. Vinyl pools need smaller amounts of chlorine more regularly to avoid bleaching the liner. You can

Swimming Pool Maintenance Made Easy

still add the algaecide with the chlorine in addition to regular skimming and brushing. Just be sure not to add more than one gallon of liquid chlorine per 10,000 gallons of water at any time. Furthermore, only add more chlorine at that rate if the chlorine has gone back down to zero.

Freezing Conditions

Colder climate pools would have been winterized and need to be "opened" in late spring to prepare them for the summer season. These pools are always covered and depending on the area, they have the plumbing drained and sometimes an antifreeze added to the pumps and lines. Follow these steps to reverse this process.

- Drain the water off of the cover

- Fold the cover as you remove it. If you have an area large enough you can thoroughly clean and dry the cover before folding and storage.

- Remove the winter plugs from all of the return lines and jets

- Remove the ice compensator (Gizmo) from the skimmers. Put the skimmer baskets back in the skimmers.

- Remove the drain plugs from the pumps to remove anti-freeze if it was used. Flush the pump with water and put the drain plugs back in. Look at the O-rings in the drain plugs first to see if they need to be replaced. Do the same

Swimming Pool Maintenance Made Easy

for the filter, heater, auto chlorinator, and booster pump drain plugs.

- Re-install the pressure gauge on your filter and any other parts that were removed from the pool.
- Adjust any valve back to normal operating position before running equipment.
- Fill pool to halfway up the tile line or skimmer opening.
- Reinstall the automatic pool cleaner in the pool.
- Add water to the pump housing by removing the lid and adding water there. Check the pump lid O-ring and replace if needed. Tighten the lid by hand.
- Open the air bleed valve on top of the filter.
- Turn the pool filter pump on. After the pump begins to prime you will feel air coming from the air bleed valve on top of the filter. After all the air is gone you will see water come from the same valve. You can then close the air bleed valve.
- You can now start the spring startup as listed above depending on the water condition.

Swimming Pool Maintenance Made Easy

Summer Season Maintenance

The hot summer heat is why we all have pools in the first place. Unfortunately the summer heat and sunlight make your pool prone to many problems this time of year. If a pool is not watched closely all summer long you will have issues like algae and loss of time you can use your pool. There are several things you can do on a weekly basis to prevent these undesired consequences.

- Perform "Weekly Tasks" above and...

- Keep chlorine levels higher (between 3-5 ppm.)

- Keep the pH maintained between 7.4 -7.6

- Maintain Alkalinity between 80 -120 (Gunite/Plaster/Pebble Tech pools) and 100 -140 (Vinyl or Fiberglass pools)

- Use tablet chlorine in floater (2 per week per 20,000 gallons)

- Keep your eye out for any algae. If you spot any at all you should consider adding an algaecide to stop it before it is a lot more difficult to remove. I use the "algaecide 60" at this point. Don't forget to brush the algae off of the walls and keep the chlorine levels at 5 ppm. A dose of 14-17 oz. per 10,000 gallons is typical (read dosage on the side of the algaecide you use). More information in the section "killing green algae".

Swimming Pool Maintenance Made Easy

- Add salt to the pool water if you have a salt pool. Have the water tested for the current salt levels and dose the pool accordingly. Each bag of pool salt will have a dosage chart on it. Most 20,000 gallon pools need 2-4 bags of pool salt per year.

- Clean the salt cell if you have one. See "cleaning the salt cell" for more info.

- Watch the water level carefully. **Never let the water level get too low.** It is dangerous for the pool pumps to run without water going through them, you can easily damage the seal in the pump. The pool will have algae issues if the equipment is not running properly.

- Run the pool the right number of hours per day. Running the pool too little will cause algae over time. Small particles can be found in the water that should be filtered out. These particles are food for algae. Think of a pool that does not run enough per day as having water with fertilizer in it. Most pools need to run between 6 and 10 hours per day depending on the pump and filter combination. There is more information below about finding out the number of hours you will need to run your particular pool.

- Clean the filter often, but not too often. Any time the pressure rises 8-10 lbs. over the starting pressure the filter should be cleaned. Cleaning the filter ensures you are moving the most water per hour and that the water is as clean as it can be. **Large cartridge filters usually only need cleaning two times per year, Spring and Fall.** Sand

Swimming Pool Maintenance Made Easy

or Diatomaceous Earth filters need cleaning more often. The amount of cleaning will depend on the filter pressure rise as described above. Cartridge filters work by removing large particles first and then smaller and smaller particles over time. Cleaning them too often will result in a dirtier and harder to maintain pool. Every spring and fall, or every time the filter pressure rises 8-10 lbs above the clean starting pressure, are two good ways to decide when to clean the cartridge style filter.

- Retest the calcium hardness and conditioner levels in the beginning and the middle of the summer. This will keep the pool surface protected and minimize the loss of chlorine do to a low conditioner level. Please also read the section called "Too Much Conditioner".

- Check the phosphate level at least once per month. High levels of phosphates contribute to a pool that is very prone to get algae. Slowly removing some of the phosphates with a phosphate remover will minimize your algae issues. Keeping your filter clean and removing debris promptly will also minimize phosphate levels without the need for a phosphate remover. **Please read my disclaimer on phosphate removers below.** To be 100% honest, I do not personally use phosphate removers in the pools that I maintain. I do have to talk about them because there are people that love them and have great results.

- Use a preventative algaecide. **"Algaecide 60" is the best algaecide to use.** You can use a maintenance dose as much as weekly during the summer to prevent algae. This

Swimming Pool Maintenance Made Easy

algaecide is inexpensive and you will not notice it in the water by smell or taste. It does not foam. **I absolutely love this algaecide.** I use it to kill algae when I see it in all of the pools that I maintain. Not all algaecides are the same, not even close. Algaecides sold at department stores or home improvement stores may be cheaper but they will not work like this algaecide. I will put a link on my website to the correct algaecide for purchase online. If you are buying algaecide locally, look for "poly oxyethylene(dimethyliminio)ethylene(dimethyliminio)ethylene dichloride 60%" as the ingredient. I call it Poly Oxyethylene 60 or algaecide 60 for short.

- Empty all baskets and pool cleaner bags weekly. Keeping these clean will minimize the amount of debris making its way to the filter. That will reduce the number of times per year you will have to clean your pool filter.

- Skim the top and bottom of the pool with a good pool net. Keeping the pool clean is more enticing to use and it minimizes any algae issues.

- Brush the pool walls every other week. You may not notice but dirt and small amounts of algae will form on your pool walls over time. If you brush the walls with a nylon brush a couple times per month you will prevent many algae issues and most staining that can develop over time.

- Shock the pool as needed. Swimmers during the summer months add a lot of contaminates to the pool water. The average active swimmer can sweat over one pint of sweat

Swimming Pool Maintenance Made Easy

per hour. Gross right? That is just one of the many contaminates introduced by swimmers alone. The list goes on and on. Shocking the pool will oxidize (or burn up) all of these contaminates, leaving the water clear and sparkling. See "Shocking the pool" for more information below.

Swimming Pool Maintenance Made Easy

Fall Pool Maintenance

Fall is in my eyes the most difficult season because the weather is unpredictable and the added leaves make things tough. People tend to start neglecting their pool after the long summer because they are no longer using the pool. Do your best to keep your pool clean and you will avoid an unnecessary and costly clean-up. Here are the other important tasks for Fall.

- Continue to Perform "Weekly Tasks" above and...

- Maintain chlorine levels between 1-3 ppm.

- Maintain pH levels between 7.4 -7.6

- Maintain Alkalinity between 80 -120 (Gunite/Plaster/Pebble Tech pools) and 100 -140 (Vinyl or Fiberglass pools)

- Stop using tablet chlorine. Remove the floating chlorinator and keep it out of the sunlight for the off season. Tablet chorine does not dissolve well in the cold water and you will be able to easily keep the right amount of chlorine in the water without this device in the pool. The other reason for not using tablet chorine all year long is that tablet chorine is high in conditioner and you will end up with too high of a level forcing you to drain some of your pool water to dilute the conditioner levels.

- Keep an eye on the water level. It is sometimes still hot and the wind that is typical of this season will evaporate water at a higher rate than just the hot sun alone. Water

Swimming Pool Maintenance Made Easy

level is very important for the pool equipment and the pool water quality equally.

- Keep the filter run time the same as the summer run time. With all the extra debris entering the pool it is important to run the filter enough. Keeping this material out of the pool water will prevent algae that will still form this time of year.

- Clean the salt cell if you have one. See "cleaning the salt cell" for more info.

- Clean the filter one more time. All the oils, suntan lotions, sweat, dirt, and detergents that entered the pool during the summer need to be removed from the filter at this time. It can help to soak the filter elements in automatic dishwasher liquid and water. Add about half a box of inexpensive automatic dishwasher detergent (not dish soap) to a large bucket of water. Soak the filter cartridges for about 8 hours in this solution. It may be necessary to turn the filters upside down and rotate each filter element into the solution if you don't have a large bucket. Rinse the elements with water before putting the filter back together again.

- Keep the pool as clean as possible. Don't let the leaves accumulate on the bottom of the pool. Remove them as soon as you can. The leaves will decompose in the pool water and contribute to pool problems over the winter and even next year. The leaves can also stain the bottom of the pool.

Swimming Pool Maintenance Made Easy

- Use a sequestering agent to prevent stains on the pool surface. Most pool stores have this product at a minimal cost. One quart usually treats the average size pool. I will put a link at mypoolmadeeasy.com for a good stain preventative.

- Drain the pool solar and shut the solar valves. If you are unsure of how to do this properly you can hire a solar company to both turn on and shut off the solar. Usually one cost per year and they will come out twice. Solar valves and plumbing are different for each pool even though there are many similarities, trying to give advice on start up and closure should be given on an individual pool specifically. It might be in your best interest to hire a solar company at least once and watch what they do if you are interested in doing it yourself in the future. Most solar companies also look for and fix leaks on the panels themselves each spring. It may be worth the cost to have one come out.

Swimming Pool Maintenance Made Easy

Winter Pool Maintenance

Please don't ignore the pool for the winter time. It is by far the most common thing that I see because it is so easy to do. Your pool will not need anywhere near as much of your time as the rest of the year. Try to maintain your pool like any other season and you will be off to a great start for next year. Here are some helpful tips. This information does not apply to areas with extreme freezing conditions. More about that below.

- Perform "Weekly Tasks" above and...

- Maintain chlorine levels between 1-3 ppm.

- Maintain pH levels between 7.4 -7.6

- Maintain Alkalinity between 80 -120 (Gunite/Plaster/Pebble Tech pools) and 100 -140 (Vinyl or Fiberglass pools)

- No tablet chlorine needed or desired during winter

- Lower the run time of your pool filter. Most pool run times can be reduced by 30-40%. The average run time during the winter after the fall leaves are gone is about 4 hours per day.

- Change the run time to run during the night and early morning hours. Just before the sun comes up is the coldest time of night. Moving water will not freeze so running the pool during these hours will protect your pool equipment and plumbing. Most variable speed pumps have a freeze

Swimming Pool Maintenance Made Easy

sensor and will automatically run at a low speed all night long regardless of the scheduled run time to prevent freezing pipes or equipment. This does not apply to areas with extreme freezing conditions.

- Clean the salt cell if you have one. See "cleaning the salt cell" for more info.

- Clean the pool filter. The pressure might still go up. Especially after rain that brings in a lot of dirt and debris from surrounding trees and yard. It is important to keep the filter pressure down. This also gives you a great chance of having a great start to next year's easy pool maintenance.

- Clean the yard around the pool. Remove any leaves that might wash into the pool during the rainy season.

- Fix any drainage issues before the rain starts. Over the years I have had a dozen or so pools that have drainage issues in the yard around the pool. When dirt washes into the pool it turns the pool brown or green almost overnight. This is not algae, it is dirt or leaves causing a teabag affect. The big problem with letting this happen is that it is very tough on your pool filter to remove all of this from the pool water. It will often damage the pool filter elements by plugging the small pores which will dramatically shorten their lives. It may also take two or more months to clear the pool and a lot of effort.

- Keep all baskets and bags clean.

Swimming Pool Maintenance Made Easy

- Keep the debris and worms off the bottom of the pool. Staining will occur if you ignore your pool this time of year.

- Lower water level if it gets too high. If the water level goes over the top of the tile you can loosen the pool tile. If it gets too cold at night and the water is behind the tile you may lose many tile. If the water goes over the top of the pool you are likely to wash a lot of debris and dirt into the pool causing more work for you. There is a drain that looks like a garden hose spigot on the pool plumbing. Attach a garden hose to that valve and turn the pump on. Open the valve and you will begin draining the pool. Don't forget to set a timer! Most pools drain by about 1 inch per 30 minutes using this method. If your pool does not have a spigot on the pool plumbing, you will need to buy a small sump pump attached to a garden hose and remove excess water that way.

Special Situations

Vinyl Pool

In ground vinyl swimming pools do not need special considerations. Above ground vinyl pools are often covered for the winter. If you are planning to cover your above ground pool there are some tricks you can learn that will give you better results.

Swimming Pool Maintenance Made Easy

First, choose your pool cover. There are different qualities of winter covers available. There are very inexpensive and thin covers and very thick long lasting ones. All covers for above ground pools have a cable that goes around the outside of the cover and tightens around the top rim of the pool. Before you cover the pool there are some things you should do.

Test the pool water and make sure the chlorine is high (3 - 5ppm.) and the pH is 7.5. Add one quart of "algaecide 60" for up to 25,000 gallons of pool water with the pump on. Let the pump run for at least 3 hours.

Buy one or more large air pillows for the center of the pool to raise the middle and cause the rain water to run off of the pool automatically. This will save you a ton of time removing both water and wet leafs all winter long.

Drape the cover over the air pillows and attach the cable. Turn the pool equipment off for the winter.

Winterizing Your Pool - Warm Climates

If you live in a place similar to California where the weather gets into the 100's in the summer and down to the low 30's and 40's

Swimming Pool Maintenance Made Easy

during the winter, you can choose to cover your pool after the swim season is complete and re-open the pool in spring.

This method is called "Winterizing" your pool. The goal is to completely cover your pool with a quality winter cover so no rain, dirt, or sunlight can enter the swimming pool. The benefit is that you will not need to run your pool equipment as much and you will save money on chemicals and electricity. The use of water bags or sandbags is necessary to hold the cover in place. The cover will collect leaves and rain water on top of it so you will also need to keep the top of the cover clean and mostly dry throughout the winter. We chemically threat the water before you cover the pool and if everything goes well, you will open the pool and find a clear, clean swimming pool. I don't personally cover the pools that I maintain or my pool at home because I find it easier and more aesthetically pleasing to keep the pools uncovered. The cost to maintain your pool in the winter is minimal. If you have a lot of trees around your pool you might give it a shot. Safety covers are also an option (described later)

Step 1

Balance the pool water. Make sure your chorine level is at 3.0 ppm. and your pH is at 7.4 - 7.6. It is also important to make sure you have no algae in the pool to start with. **If there is algae you need to take the steps and the time to remove it first or you may open the pool in the spring to a green pool** (follow the section called "Killing Green Algae").

Step 2

Add a preventative algaecide. If you do not see any algae in the pool water you will not be shocking the pool and using an

Swimming Pool Maintenance Made Easy

algaecide like you will if you did. It is still best to add a full dose of algaecide as a preventative before you cover the pool. Please add 14-17 oz. per 10,000 gallons, of "algaecide 60" (60% Poly (oxyethlene (dimethyliminio) ethylene) available at any pool store or online (link at mtpoolmadeeasy.com)

Step 3

Fill the pool to near the top of the tile. It is still important to maintain a normal or high water level during the off season with the cover on. You will still be running the pool equipment at times and it is easier to keep the top of the cover clean if the cover is not too far down inside the pool. The cover will float on the water so raising the water level in the pool up a little will raise the cover. You do not want to raise the level of the water above the top of the tile at any time.

Step 4

Cover the pool. Make sure you are buying a quality winter cover designed for your pool. Most good winter covers are two or three layers thick, usually blue on one side and black on the other. They are designed to block all sunlight and do not allow water to penetrate the cover. You will buy a cover big enough to extend at least 3' beyond the edges of the pool. This is because you will be using water or sand bags all around the pool to hold the cover firmly to the ground throughout the winter.

On the typical cover the blue side goes up. Open the cover over the pool and put weights in the four corners until you have had time to add water to the water bags. Make sure the cover is not resting on anything sharp like a rock or boulder. The cover will move some when the wind blows and you are sure to end up with

Swimming Pool Maintenance Made Easy

a hole in the cover. If you do need to put the cover over rocks or boulders you should consider laying a thick tarp over the rocks first to avoid tears in the expensive winter cover. If the cover is too long in some areas it may be necessary to fold the cover under itself to fit your pool better. It is better to have the water or sand bags between 1' and 2' away from the pool edge.

Step 5

Lay the water bags down on top of the cover that is resting on the deck of your pool and fill them with water. As noted above, try to place the bags somewhat close to the pool edge and follow the shape of the pool as much as possible. This will make the cleaning and maintenance of the cover easier. You can purchase different size and shape water bags to meet your individual needs. You will need to have the bags almost touching end to end all the way around the pool to secure the cover. Some choose to leave a space of up to 18" between each water bag to save money and time. Do not attempt this if you live in a windy area. The use of "air pillows" are not needed for in ground pools.

Step 6

Reduce or turn off pool equipment. If you do not live where the temperatures fall below freezing for long periods of time (more than 6 hours), you can turn off or greatly reduce the number of hours your pool filter pump runs per day. You can also turn off the booster pump. This will save you hundreds of dollars in energy costs while the cover is on the pool. You will still need to run the pump a few hours per month after you check under the cover to see if chemicals are needed (about once a month). When a "hard freeze" or "overnight freeze warning" are forecasted you have

Swimming Pool Maintenance Made Easy

the option of running your pool pump during the night to avoid any pipes from freezing. If you have a multi speed pump (Variable Speed) you only need to run the pump in a lower speed. Moving water does not freeze at these temperatures. **Make sure the water level in your pool has not dropped before running the pool equipment.**

Congratulations, your pool is now winterized. **You will still need to maintain the cover and the pool water; we will go over those topics now.**

Keep the Cover Clean and Dry

It is important to keep the cover as dry as possible. More important, you cannot let the water build up on the cover because you are risking the cover being pulled into the pool. If the water level under the cover goes down and you don't fill it back up again this will happen very easily. You don't want this to happen because the cover will be very heavy and probably dirty. All of the dirt and debris will now be in your pool and you will need to start all over again to put the cover back on the pool. Any pool store sells a drain that you can use to remove the water off of the top of the cover. You can buy a small sump pump that you attach a garden hose too and pump the water off the cover as well. Your pool store should be able to show you the options they have available.

Check the Water Balance Once Per Month

The chemical levels are still important this time of year. Adding a cover does prevent most chlorine loss and pH change unless

Swimming Pool Maintenance Made Easy

water and debris find a way into your pool. It is best to check those levels at least once per month to avoid a dirty pool when you uncover it in the spring. Peel back a corner of the pool cover to test water and add chemicals if needed. It is best to do this near one of the return lines (the water going back to the pool) so that when you add chemicals they are jettisoned into the pool. Keep the chlorine at 1-3ppm and the pH between 7.4 and 7.6. If you need to add a chemical, turn the filter pump on first and let it run for a minimum of 3 hours. You may go through an entire winter and never need to add any extra chemicals but it is best to check.

Remove the Cover Early

It is best to remove the cover around March or April at the latest. This is because you will have time to clean the pool before the swim season and because you do not want the winter cover on the pool when it starts to get hot. The top of the cover will start to grow difficult to remove algae and the pool itself will most likely have a few issues starting with algae. It is better if you can see the pool to avoid those issues.

You will need to clean the cover the best you can before removing the water bags and pulling the cover off. This is because you do not want all that dirt and water to enter the pool when you are removing the cover.

Remove the water bags by draining and cleaning each one. Allow to dry and then store them in a cool dry place such as your garage or shed. Do not allow them to be exposed to the sun during the summer or you will be replacing them next winter.

Swimming Pool Maintenance Made Easy

Remove the cover by pulling it off of the pool. You will need to clean the cover before storing it. Most pool store sell a cover cleaner that you can use. Follow the label instructions on the product you buy. You can also hose off the cover and rotate the cover on the ground until it is dry and can be stored. You do not want to put the cover away dirty or wet. Mold and algae will grow and the cover may not be usable next year. Store the cover in a cool and dry place. You can cover the pool cover with a tarp to keep dirt off of it.

Winterizing Pool - Freezing Conditions

Winterizing your pool in a cold weather climate is a lot different than warm weather conditions (barely freezing winter).

There are several steps you will need to take to winterize your pool properly (Freezing Conditions).

1. Test the pool water to insure the chlorine level is between 3-5 ppm. The pH should be between 7.4 - 7.6.
2. Clean the pool filter.
3. Add one quart of "algaecide 60" (60% Poly (oxyethlene (dimethyliminio) ethylene) for 25,000 gallons of pool water. Run the pool pump for about 5 hours.
4. Lower the water level below the skimmer and all return lines (normally about 18 inches below the tile line). You can

Swimming Pool Maintenance Made Easy

also purchase a "blowout extension" to remove water from the lines.

5. Remove the drain plugs from the pump strainer basket housing, the pump volute, the filter tank, and the heater. Make sure you keep the drain plugs safe. You will need them again.

6. Remove the pressure relief valve and pressure gauge from the top of the filter.

7. Drain the booster pump and the automatic chlorinator, if you have one.

8. Shut the breakers off for all pool equipment.

9. Position the multi-port valve handle between any two settings. This will ensure all ports are partially open to allow for freeze expansion.

10. When the water has completely drained out of the plumbing lines, put winterizing plugs into the return lines and skimmer lines.

11. Add pool antifreeze to all lines. Antifreeze should be added at the rate of 1 gallon per 10 feet of pipe (average product requirements).

12. Place a "**Gizmo**" into the skimmer to seal the skimmer pipe and absorb any ice pressure.

13. Refill the pool back to between 4-6 inches below the skimmer inlet in vinyl-lined pools or 4-6 inches

Swimming Pool Maintenance Made Easy

below the tile line plaster pools.

14. Remove all ladders, hoses, over-the-top skimmers, etc. If you have an automatic pool cleaner, remove it and drain it completely. Lay the hoses out straight in a non-freezing location.

15. Cover the pool with the best winter cover you can find. You will need to keep the cover clean and keep the water off of the cover throughout the winter.

16. Add water bags or sand bags around the edge of the pool on top of the winter cover. In normal conditions, these can be placed 18 inches apart, but in windy areas, they should be placed end-to-end.

Swimming Pool Maintenance Made Easy

Getting down to basics

I know that when you look at all of the things that are needed to maintain a swimming pool it can feel a little overwhelming. I can only tell you that after you have done it for a while it becomes second nature. My hope is that I can fully explain each task below to help you learn what you need to know.

Testing the Pool Water

Pool chemistry is probably the most feared part of pool maintenance. Most people think that there is too much to learn and it is not possible without professional help. I will tell you that that is both right and wrong. There is a lot that you can choose to learn about your pool waters chemistry, or you can choose to learn the most important parts only. Either way, after you understand it you will feel comfortable testing and adding the right chemicals to your pool to keep it shiny and blue (healthy too).

The Easy Part
Weekly testing of chlorine, pH, and total alkalinity is needed to make sure your water stays beautiful, healthy, and comfortable too. Testing the water can be done with different tools and after you get the hang of it, it only takes about 3 minutes to do.

Swimming Pool Maintenance Made Easy

What type of test kit to use

There are several methods for testing pool water. Test strips are easy to use but are not very accurate (you can do the same test a few times in a row and get different results). The drop kits are the most accurate and are not difficult to use after a quick explanation.

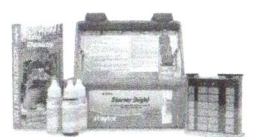

There are two different types of drop kits available at any pool store or online. The first is labeled an "Oto" test kit. If you open the kit you will notice the test block will have yellow for the chlorine side and red for the pH side. This kit is fine but not my favorite. The chlorine side will only test "total chlorine" (which we really want to know the "Free" chlorine instead). The second kit is a "Dpd" test kit. You will notice the chlorine side of the kit has shades of red as well as the pH side. This kit will test both "free" chlorine and "total" chlorine. "Free" chlorine is chlorine that has not combined itself with any other particles in the water and is just sitting there waiting to be needed.

Swimming Pool Maintenance Made Easy

Ideal Ranges

Chlorine - acceptable range is from 1 ppm to 5 ppm. The ideal range for a clean and easy to maintain pool is between 3 ppm and 5 ppm.

pH - acceptable range is from 7.2 - 7.8. The ideal range is from 7.4 - 7.6.

Alkalinity - acceptable range is rom 80 - 120 for plaster or pebble tech pools and from 100 - 140 for vinyl or fiberglass pools.

Calcium Hardness - Ideal range 200 - 400 ppm

Conditioner - Ideal range 50 - 80 ppm

Phosphate - Lower than 300 - 500 ppb is best

Total Dissolved Solids - Ideal range is under 1500 ppm (unless you have a salt pool)

Testing the Chlorine

In this book we will talk about the "Dpd" testing kit.

The chlorine test is on the left. Fill the test block with your pool water up to the fill line on the kit. Follow the directions on the kit. Most often you put 5 drops of number 1 into the left side, and then 5 drops of number 2 into the same side. Then you cap it and shake it for a second. Hold the kit up to the light or a light background any you should be able to tell what shade your water

Swimming Pool Maintenance Made Easy

matches compared to the different colors next to it. Just try to pick the one that most closely matches your water. Read the number next to the color. That is your free chlorine level. You will not need to test the "total chlorine" unless you have a strong chlorine smell to the water or are having problems with algae. To test the "total chlorine" leave the water you just tested in the kit and add 5 drops of number 3. Cap it and shake it. If the color did not change then all of your chlorine is "free" and ready to work. If the reading went up by 1 ppm for instance, then you have combined chlorine of 1 ppm. You will need to shock the pool with extra chlorine to get rid of the combined chlorine. We will talk about what to do about that under "shocking your pool".

The ideal chlorine levels are between 1 and 5 ppm. depending on the season and the water quality.

Testing the pH

The pH test is on the right of the testing block. Fill the block the same as the chlorine side (you can do these tests at the same time of course). Put 5 drops of the pH reagent (usually number 4) into the water to be tested. Cap and shake. Try to match your water to the closest color on the testing block. The ideal range for pH is 7.4 - 7.6. Acceptable range is 7.2 - 7.8. Below you will learn what to do when these levels are off.

Some of the more advanced kits have a testing bottle for "Acid Demand" and one for "Base Demand". If the pH is not within its normal range you can run an additional test. Keep the water that is testing high or low in the testing block. Lest say the test says your pH is high (above 7.6) and you want to know how much acid

Swimming Pool Maintenance Made Easy

you need to add. Grab the "Acid Demand" dropper and start by adding one drop and then shake the kit again and look at the results. You might notice the color of the pH test changed already. Keep adding on drop at a time until the pH reads between 7.4 and 7.6. Remember how many drops it took and grab the book that came with the test kit. Inside you will find a chart that talks about acid demand. There you will find your pool gallonage and the number of drops you needed. Follow those across the chart and you will see how much acid you need to add. The same thing is true for "Base Demand". The chart will tell you how much soda ash or baking soda to add to raise a low pH to the correct level.

Testing Alkalinity

The total alkalinity test does not necessarily need to be done every week. As a rule of thumb if the pH is where we want it to be, you do not need to test the alkalinity. If the pH is not right you should test the alkalinity because they work together (more below). To test alkalinity fill the large test tube provided to the mark shown by the kit (usually 25ml). Add 2 drops of number 7 and add 5 drops of number 8. Swirl the water slowly. Then add one drop of number 9 at a time and count each drop swirling between drops. The water will go from green to red. Stop counting when it turns red completely. If it took 8 drops to turn the water red your alkalinity is 80. **I will explain what the alkalinity is and how it works in the next section.**

Testing Calcium

Most residential test kits do not test for calcium hardness. If you did buy this type of kit there are directions in the kit that you

Swimming Pool Maintenance Made Easy

should follow. I don't believe you need a kit that tests this level unless you have a leak in your pool and you are concerned that the levels are low often. Otherwise, you only need to have the calcium level tested two times per year. Spring and fall are the ideal times to have this done. Most pool stores offer a free water test. You will need to make sure that they will test for this and conditioner.

The reason that they only need to be tested two times per year is because once the levels are adjusted they change very slowly. The only way you change the calcium level is if you dilute the level down with tap water (leak) or raise it adding chemicals that have calcium as a base (calcium hypochlorite shock). I do not recommend using calcium hypochlorite shock anyway because it has the potential to leave calcium carbonate behind and possibly hurt your cartridge filters. Calcium hypochlorite is used as an inexpensive chlorine shock treatment. **I recommend sodium dichlor (granular chlorine) or liquid chlorine as a shock instead.** You will see in the next paragraph why I think liquid chlorine is ultimately the best "Shock" for your pool.

Testing Cyanuric Acid (Conditioner)

The same is true for conditioner that is true for calcium hardness; you only need to have this level tested two times per year. The level goes down by dilution (leak) and up with the use of too much trichlor (3" tabs) or sodium dichlor (granular chlorine).

Conditioner levels over 80 ppm are not needed to protect chlorine from the sunlight and may cause undesired effects including algae (more under Cyanuric Acid).

Swimming Pool Maintenance Made Easy

Ask your local pool store to test for conditioner for you. Don't hesitate to add more conditioner if your levels are low. It will be the difference of hundreds of dollars wasted on chlorine every year.

Testing Phosphate Levels

I have already mentioned briefly the way I feel about phosphates and their removal. To put it shortly, I don't use phosphate removers in the pools that I maintain or my own pool at home. My longer explanation is below in the section labeled "Phosphate Removers". With that said, some people love phosphate removers and have great results preventing algae using them on a regular basis.

There are take home phosphate test kits available at any swimming pool store. There are too many variations available to mention one style here. Follow the directions that came with the kit and test every month during the spring and weekly during the summer. Keeping a low phosphate level will reduce the amount of algae you might deal with each year. Keeping your filter clean and debris out of the pool in addition to proper number of hours per day running your filter will also minimize your phosphate levels without a chemical additive.

Phosphate levels should be maintained below 500 ppb.

If you do decide to use a phosphate remover you should have a clean filter and monitor your pressure closely. If the pressure goes up by 8 - 10 lbs. you will need to clean the filter again. Phosphates are always being introduced to the pool so monthly or weekly monitoring would be needed.

Swimming Pool Maintenance Made Easy

As mentioned, I personally do not use phosphate removers on the pools I maintain. I think that it should be reserved for pools with continual algae issues with the understanding that the filters will need more attention (cleaning).

Testing Total Dissolved Solids

The total dissolved solids level is the one test that is only needed if you are concerned about how old the water is in regards to how many chemicals have ever been added to the water and any waste products left behind from swimmers (lotions, oils, sweat, and so on). Only a swimming pool store might have the test device required for this test. The device costs over $400 so many stores will not have one. The test literally tells you how many "dissolved solids" or chemicals or material that were solid (granular, tabs, other chlorine, and swimmer waste) and have now dissolved into the water and is now part of the water. It is possible that if you have a very high use pool or an average use spa that you end up with more dissolved solids than water. I'm just kidding about the "More" part but you have to agree that it does illustrate the point that it would be pretty gross to leave oversaturated water in your pool or spa and continue to swim/bathe.

If you were having a lot of issues with the chlorine not performing well or doing its job, you may want to have this level tested. If the total dissolved solids level is over 1500 ppm, you may need to drain part of your pool water and add new water to dilute it down.

Swimming Pool Maintenance Made Easy

For the most part, no one needs to worry about this test. Most pools loose enough water through evaporation to keep TDS low. It's kind of a, last resort to find a problem, kind of test. A side note; if you use salt you will have a high total dissolved solids level and this test cannot help you.

Everything You are Testing and Why

Proper chemical balance can mean the difference between an easy to maintain and long lasting beautiful swimming pool and a difficult to maintain, short lived and ugly pool.

Too much chlorine can irritate the skin and eyes by drying them out. Too little or no chlorine will cause algae, bacteria, and viruses to take over your pool.

The pH is very important for a couple reasons.

The first is for you and the second is for your pool. A pH in the ideal range is closest to the pH of your eyes and skin and therefore makes the water less irritating. Rashes can form as well as red eyes when the pH is not right. Most blame the chlorine for this. It is possible that combined chlorine is the cause for eye and skin irritation too.

The pool needs a balanced pH for the pool surface, plumbing, and pool equipment to last and not cause damage.

Swimming Pool Maintenance Made Easy

A low pH (under 7.2) is a little too acidic and slowly eats away at pool plaster, pipes, and metal components in the pool equipment.

Too high of a pH is scale forming. That means that you can cause calcium and other minerals from the water to come out of the water and form on the walls and everything else including your filter. These are some of the biggest reasons some pools look more stained than others of the same age.

Alkalinity is a buffer for the pH. That means that if the alkalinity level is low then the pH bounces all over the place but if the alkalinity is high the pH is locked in. Too much either way is not good. Don't worry; it is rare that you ever have to worry about the alkalinity because balancing the pH usually keeps the alkalinity levels perfect. You just need to test the alkalinity to be sure. If you are constantly needing to change the level of your pH, the alkalinity level is probably low. You can test it and raise the level to 80 - 120 ppm (Gunite, Plaster, or Pebble Tech Pools) and 100 -140 ppm (Vinyl or Fiberglass Pools) so that your pH doesn't fluctuate so rapidly.

Calcium Hardness is very important to check at least two times per year because a low level can mean that the pool water will pull the calcium that it needs to balance itself from the pool walls itself. Over time the pool walls will be void of very important calcium and will become very rough and begin to degrade. There are also problems with calcium levels that are too high. It is possible with a high calcium hardness level combined with a high pH and alkalinity; you can knock the calcium out of suspension and precipitate it out onto the walls and tile. That means that the calcium leaves the water and forms on the walls

Swimming Pool Maintenance Made Easy

leaving a rough and almost sharp formation that would need to be acid washed or sanded off. There is a very wide ideal range of 200-400 ppm. and acceptable range of 150-500 ppm..

Conditioner (Cyanuric Acid) is needed to protect the chlorine from the sunlight. **Think of it as a sunscreen for the chlorine.**

The minimum level of conditioner required to protect the chlorine is 30 ppm. Just an interesting side note, if you did not have any conditioner in the water you will lose 100% of your chlorine after only 8 hours of sunlight. The ideal range for a residential pool is 50 - 80 ppm. **I keep all of the pools that I maintain at 60ppm conditioner.**

The higher the conditioner level, the more chlorine you will need to sanitize your pool water or kill algae, bacteria, or viruses. The best and easiest way that I can describe why this is true is to give you a visualization. Picture one chorine molecule surrounded by 60 conditioner molecules to protect it from the sunlight. The chlorine can still do its job. If you surround that same (and every) chlorine molecule by 100+ conditioner molecules, it becomes harder and harder for the chlorine to do its job. This means that you will need many more chlorine molecules to kill all of the bad things that you do not want in your pool. Sometimes 3-5 times more chlorine would be needed. I doubt you want that much chlorine in your pool either.

The fact that we have to add chlorine about once per week in the summer is actually a good thing. When you add chlorine to pool water by way of liquid, granular, or shock, you are doing more than just raising the chlorine level. You are actually oxidizing the water as well. When you oxidize the water you burn up the contaminates (lotions, oils, sweat, urine, dirt, decayed leaves) that have combined themselves with old chlorine molecules (combined chlorine). **Combined chlorine is a weak sanitizer that causes eye and skin irritation and has a strong odor you might remember from a public pool during your childhood.** Combined chlorine is also called chloramine. In fact, public pools need to oxidize their water at such a high rate they are only allowed to keep conditioner levels as high as 50 ppm. This ensures they replace chlorine constantly and heavily oxidize the water. So if you keep your levels below 80 ppm. but over 50 ppm. you will do great. As I said before, I shoot for 60 ppm on all of the pools that I maintain.

Swimming Pool Maintenance Made Easy

How to Adjust your Chemical Levels

Okay, here comes the fun part! This is where most people are afraid to get involved. I understand where those fear come from. You might be concerned that you will do something wrong that will either cost you money now to correct a mistake, or a lot more later from possible damage to your pool.

The truth is that most of the levels we talked about only need to be balanced two times per year and you can always ask your local pool store for help if you need it. The other levels that you will be changing weekly are very easy to get used to if you test your pool weekly.

Test Weekly

Chlorine

pH

Alkalinity

Phosphate (If testing)

Test Two Times Per Year

Calcium

Conditioner

Total Dissolved Solids (Only if you think your water is too "Old")

Swimming Pool Maintenance Made Easy

Ideal Ranges

Chlorine - acceptable range is from 1 ppm to 5 ppm. The ideal range for a clean and easy to maintain pool is between 3 ppm and 5 ppm.

pH - acceptable range is from 7.2 – 7.8. The ideal range is from 7.4 – 7.6.

Alkalinity - acceptable range is rom 80 – 120 for plaster pools and from 100 – 140 for vinyl or fiberglass pools.

Calcium Hardness – Ideal range 200 – 400 ppm

Conditioner – Ideal range 50 -80 ppm

Phosphate – Lower than 500 ppb is best

Total Dissolved Solids – Ideal range is under 1500 ppm (unless salt pool)

Swimming Pool Maintenance Made Easy

Adding Chlorine

How much chlorine do I need to add and what type should I use? There are a few things to consider.

What is the current chlorine reading?

What condition is the water in?

Are you fighting any algae in your pool right now?

If the water is very clear and there are no algae, very little chlorine will be needed to maintain your pool. Normal free chlorine reading of 1-5ppm will keep things nice as long as you keep the filter clean and run the pump the correct number of hours per day. We will go over all of that soon. You can follow the standard chart below for dosage instructions based on your pools calculated gallonage.

If the pool is slightly cloudy or has the start of algae in a few corners of your pool or on one wall (usually the shady wall), you will need a chorine level of at least 5ppm and a lot more filter running until the pool is clear. You will also want to use some algaecide and brush the pool to make sure you kill the algae before it gets a strong start in your pool. I like to use algaecide 60 right after you raise the chlorine and brush all of the walls. Add the algaecide and run the pump for 8 hours. Your pool will be sparkling in a few days. Don't forget to retest your chlorine and pH regularly because when the algaecide works the chlorine is

Swimming Pool Maintenance Made Easy

often used up to kill the algae. You can then dose the pool using the chart below to achieve normal levels.

If the pool went completely green see the section explaining how to kill green algae. The trick is to never let your pool look like that. It is easier to prevent than you might think.

Types of Chlorine

Liquid Chlorine is the easiest to add (pour slow so you don't splash) and the least expensive to buy. It does not last very long on the shelf so don't buy too much. Typical liquid chlorine will last only 45 days full strength and loses strength every week after that. Most likely near worthless after 6 months. There is a dosage chart below. Liquid chlorine is my favorite chlorine and the type that I add most often. This is because it causes the least number of undesired effects to the water. Liquid chlorine is made with sodium and not calcium. This means it will not raise the calcium levels in your pool. It is also not a stabilized chlorine. Stabilizer is another word for conditioner or cyanuric acid. Remember the section above about too much conditioner in a pool and its negative effects.

All of this means that you can add liquid chlorine without worrying about raising other levels that you will have to deal with later by draining part of your pool to dilute the levels down. There is one level that liquid chlorine will change. Liquid chlorine raises the pH. Every gallon of liquid chlorine that you add will

Swimming Pool Maintenance Made Easy

technically require one quart of acid to counter the change in pH. With that said, I don't add one quart of acid every time I add liquid chlorine. I just keep my eye on the pH and adjust it as needed. I will however add acid if the pH is already borderline high and I also need chlorine. I will add the acid first with the pump on and then a few minutes later I will add my chlorine.

Tablet chorine is the strongest form of chlorine and very slow dissolving. It is a great chlorine to put in a floating chlorinator or automatic chlorinator (over by the pool equipment) if there is one. You only need between 1-2 tablets (3") per week for the average pool. Tablet chlorine is only used to try and hold a chlorine level where it is. It is not used to raise a level because they do not dissolve fast enough for that. Most pool owners use tablet chlorine to help out during the summer months. The tabs just don't dissolve well in the cold water anyway and are not needed. If you use tab chlorine you will still need liquid or granular chlorine to raise chlorine levels.

I personally use tablet chlorine from about April through September. I do not use tabs the rest of the year primarily because they are made of about 40% conditioner. This means that they raise your conditioner levels pretty quickly. If you use them all year long you will most definitely need to drain your pool when the conditioner levels get too high. Tabs also effect the pH but in the opposite direction as liquid chlorine. This actually works out to be good during the summer when you are adding liquid chlorine to raise a chlorine level that is low and tabs to maintain that level for longer. They mostly cancel each others pH

Swimming Pool Maintenance Made Easy

changes so you will not need to constantly change the pH to keep it in range.

Granular chlorine is available in two forms. Look at the ingredients before you buy. You want to buy "sodium dichloro-s-triazinetrione" not "calcium hypochlorite". The calcium chlorine leaves a byproduct behind called calcium carbonate that can bond to the filters and shorten their lives. I never use Calcium Hypochlorite. It is the cheapest and most widely available granular chlorine. It is sold at pool stores and department stores alike. It is also the strongest chlorine besides tabs. I still won't use it. I have seen it do too much damage.

Sodium dichlor chlorine is also made with up to 40% conditioner like tablet chlorine. We talked a little about conditioner above. You don't want the conditioner levels to build up too high so use this chlorine sparingly if at all. I really prefer liquid chlorine. I will however use this chlorine on pools that I am maintaining that have small or large leaks. Some homeowners can't immediately fix or are having problems finding the leak so quite a lot of time goes by. If I only use liquid chlorine and tabs in this pool I will soon be adding conditioner due to the dilution. On a pool like this I will use tablet chlorine and Sodium Dichlor to help keep the chlorine and the conditioner levels balanced. Even on a pool with a leak I would still need to monitor the conditioner levels in case they got too high. At that point I would go back to liquid chlorine only. The pH of sodium dichlor is neutral at 7.0. This means that

Swimming Pool Maintenance Made Easy

it will not dramatically change the pH of the pool water as you add it.

How much chlorine to add?

Here is a chart you can use after you know your pool gallonage. **This chart should be used for pools that are clean and clear.** Extra chlorine may be required to achieve the same results if there are algae or cloudy water. Most algaecides require you to double these amounts of chlorine for the algaecide to be effective.

	1ppm	2ppm	3ppm	4ppm	5ppm
5,000	5.33 fl. oz.	10.70 fl. Oz.	1 pt.	1.34 pts.	1.67 pts.
10,000	10.70 fl. oz.	21.40 fl. Oz.	1 qt.	2.67 pts.	1.67 qts.
15,000	1 pt.	1 qt	1.5 qts.	½ gallon	2.5 qts.
20,000	1.33 pts.	1.33 qts.	½ gallon	2.68 qts.	3.33 qts.
25,000	1.66 pts.	1.66 qts.	2.5 qt.	3.35 qts.	4.16 qts.
30,000	1 qt.	½ gallon	3 qts.	1 gallon	1.25 gallons
35,000	1.16 qts	2.33 qts.	3.5 qts.	4.69 qts.	1.45 gallons
40,000	1.33 qts.	2.66 qts.	1 gallon	5.36 qts.	1.67 gallons

Amount of <u>**Liquid Chlorine**</u> required to raise chlorine level. First find your approximate pool gallonage and then look for how many ppm. you are trying to add to your water.

Swimming Pool Maintenance Made Easy

Amount of **Granular Chlorine** required to raise chlorine level. First find your approximate pool gallonage and then look for how many ppm. you are trying to add to your water. The same is true as above in regard to algae and algaecides. Double the chlorine amounts with the algaecide to help kill the algae.

	1ppm	2ppm	3ppm	4ppm	5ppm
5,000	1.11 oz.	2.22 oz.	3.33 oz.	4.44 oz.	5.55 oz.
10,000	2.22 oz.	4.44 oz.	6.66 oz.	8.88 oz.	11.1 oz.
15,000	3.33 oz.	6.66 oz.	9.99 oz.	13.32 oz.	1.04 lbs.
20,000	4.44 oz.	8.88 oz.	13.32 oz.	1.11 lb.	1.39 lbs.
25,000	5.55 oz.	11.1 oz.	1.04 lbs.	1.39 lbs.	1.73 lbs.
30,000	6.66 oz.	13.32 oz.	1.25 lbs.	1.67 lbs.	2.08 lbs.
35,000	7.77 oz.	15.54 oz.	1.46 lbs.	1.94 lbs.	2.43 lbs.
40,000	8.88 oz.	1.11 lbs.	1.67 lbs.	2.22 lbs.	2.67 lbs.

Measurements are by weight. If you do not have a scale, buy a 1 lb. bag of granular chlorine and add it to the container you will be using to measure out your chlorine in the future. Mark the container for a 1 lb. amount. 1 Lb. of chlorine is 16 oz. You do not need to be exact. Very close is just fine. The exact amounts listed above are for reference, you can round them up or down a little.

Swimming Pool Maintenance Made Easy

How long will the chlorine last?

That depends on the current condition of the water, chemical levels (conditioner and pH), conditions outside, water temperature, and pool equipment condition/run times.

If the pool is clear, the water temperature is less than 80 degrees, and the pool pump is running the right number of hours per day, the chlorine might last all week. If the chlorine is under a huge demand from swimmers or other contaminates that enter the pool like dirt or leaves or an underlying algae issue that you can't see yet, the chlorine might only hang around for two to three days, sometimes less. If the pool has an underlying or obvious algae issue the chlorine might last only a few hours.

This is called chlorine draw. All of the things listed above will draw on the chlorine reducing how long it will last. Almost all of those things can be easily remedied. Make sure you keep the filter clean and run the pump the correct amount of time per day. Remove all leaves and other debris as soon as possible and kill any obvious (visible) algae. If you are still going through a lot of chlorine and can't figure out why, you probably have an underlying algae that you can't see. This might be because the walls of your pool are rough and easy for algae to attach. Try shocking the pool and use the 60% algaecide. Brush the pool thoroughly and run the pump for at least 8 hours. In a few days re-adjust the chlorine levels to 3-5ppm and your chlorine demand issue might be solved. The only other chlorine draw that I didn't mention directly is the pool surface itself. Unfortunately, when the plaster surface is very old (over 15 years) and if it is rough, the material itself will draw on the chlorine as it comes off into the water. At this point it is time to resurface your pool.

Shocking the pool

When there are algae or cloudy water present, you may need to shock the pool. Shocking the pool raises the chlorine levels very high as well as oxidizes the water (burns up organic contaminates). Shocking can be accomplished with two different products.

Liquid chlorine at the rate of 1 gallon per 10,000 gallons pool water will kill or weaken most algae. Then an algaecide can be used (see killing green algae for more info). This will also clear cloudy water.

Granular chlorine (sodium or calcium) can be used at the rate of 1 to 1.5 lbs. per 10,000 gallons to do the same (dosages are on the label of the product you buy and vary slightly depending on the brand).

Swimming Pool Maintenance Made Easy

How to adjust your pH and Alkalinity

First I need to explain the relationship between the pH and Alkalinity. Don't worry, it's not too tough! Lol

The Alkalinity acts like a buffer for the pH. So if the alkalinity is low, your pH will move very easily. For instance, if your alkalinity is low (below 80ppm) and you add one gallon of liquid chlorine (which has a high pH value) the pH in the pool is very likely to go up. You may then need to add acid to lower the pH. If the alkalinity is normal (lets say 100ppm) and you add the same gallon of liquid chlorine, your pH might change slightly but probably not enough to see on a test and most likely not enough for you to have to add acid to lower it. The problem compounds because the acid you add to lower the high pH that was caused by adding the gallon of liquid chlorine while your alkalinity was low, will in turn lower your alkalinity even lower. Crazy right!?!

The opposite is true if the alkalinity level is too high. The pH will be very difficult to move, even if you want to adjust it. You will most likely need more acid to lower the pH, which luckily will also lower the alkalinity.

Alkalinity and pH will usually go up and down together.

The pH is a measure of how acidic (low) or basic (high) the water is. When the pH is too low you will need to add a base product to the pool to raise the pH level. The most common is baking soda (Sodium Bi-Carbonate). When it is too high you will need to add liquid acid (Muriatic Acid) to lower the pH. Your test kit will give

Swimming Pool Maintenance Made Easy

you a chart that tells you how much to add. You will simply find your current pH level and the gallons of your pool and follow that across on the chart.

More sophisticated test kits will give you an "acid demand" bottle and a "base demand" bottle. If the pH is not within its normal range you can run an additional test. Keep the water that is testing high or low in the testing block. Lest say the test says your pH is high (above 7.6) and you want to know how much acid you need to add. Grab the "Acid Demand" dropper and start by adding one drop and then shake the kit again and look at the results. You might notice the color of the pH test changed already. Keep adding on drop at a time until the pH reads between 7.4 and 7.6. Remember how many drops it took and grab the book that came with the test kit. Inside you will find a chart that talks about acid demand. There you will find your pool gallonage and the number of drops you needed. Follow those across the chart and you will see how much acid you need to add. The same thing is true for "Base Demand". The chart will tell you how much soda ash or baking soda to add to raise a low pH to the correct level.

The easier way to raise your pH is to test your alkalinity level and raise it. The pH will go up with it. The easy formula for adding baking soda to raise your alkalinity is 1.5 lbs. per 10,000 gallons of pool water will raise your alkalinity 10ppm.

Example: If you have a 20,000 gallon pool with an alkalinity level of 60 ppm, you will need 3 lbs. of baking soda for each 10ppm. To get to 100, you will need 12 lbs. of baking soda. This will raise your pH as well.

Swimming Pool Maintenance Made Easy

To lower your pH you should verify how high the pH and alkalinity are and add small amounts of liquid acid (muriatic acid) of about one quart every two hours with the pump running. Retest the water before adding more acid.

Note: The pool filter pump should be running anytime you are adding any pool chemical and continue to run to mix in the chemical throughout your pool for at least 2 hours (one turnover is preferred).

How to Add Acid

Adding acid can be dangerous if done improperly or carelessly. Here is what you need to know.

1. Pour acid slowly around the perimeter of the pool but in the deep end only with the pump running and not too close to any steps or swim outs.

2. Pour with your arm extended and hold the bottle close to the pool water so that you don't splash.

3. Keep walking while adding the acid and don't breath in the fumes. Sometimes there is even a cloud that you can see in the air. It will make you cough and I'm sure it isn't good for you.

4. Wash your skin immediately if you think you have any acid on it. It will start to burn and get worse quickly if you don't wash it off. I have never had it leave a mark on me but I definitely have felt it and had to run to the shallow end of the pool and wash my skin (usually leg).

Swimming Pool Maintenance Made Easy

5. Wash concrete right away if any gets onto it. It will etch the concrete leaving rough spots and stains.

6. If you are going to mix acid and water, always add the acid to the bucket of water. NEVER add water to acid!

7. Wear rubber gloves, eye protection, and a mask at least the first few times you add acid until you get the hang of how to pour it and how it splashes and so on.

8. Never mix acid with any other chemical.

9. Never add liquid acid (muriatic) to a vinyl liner pool. You should not need to lower the pH of a vinyl liner pool anyway because the pH is always going down (lower) naturally. You will almost always need to raise the pH instead (see next section). If you did have to add acid to a vinyl pool for some reason, they sell dry acid (sodium bisulfate) that you mix in a bucket of water first and that acid is not as strong as muriatic acid.

10. Be sure to keep a neutralizing agent nearby in case you accidentally spill the muriatic acid. Suitable neutralizers include pulverized garden lime, baking soda, and plain water. Sprinkle the neutralizer slowly around the edges of the **spill** and then toward the center to minimize any carbon dioxide foaming

11. Always store muriatic acid in its original container.

12. Keep muriatic acid out of the reach of children but not high up on a shelf. I recommend in a low cabinet made of plastic or wood.

Swimming Pool Maintenance Made Easy

13. If you store your acid (or chlorine) in your garage next to your beautiful bicycle, you won't have your bike for long.

14. Use common sense, it's acid. Lol

Special Situations

Vinyl Liner or Fiberglass Pools - Raising pH

Both vinyl and fiberglass pools use a different product to raise the pH. Instead of baking soda (sodium bi-carbonate) they will use soda ash (sodium carbonate). Confusing right? Let me explain.

Baking soda raises both pH and alkalinity but it raises the alkalinity more than it raises the pH. Soda ash raises both the pH and alkalinity but it raises the pH more than it raises alkalinity.

Vinyl and fiberglass pools often have their pH drop all by itself. This is because of the type of surface. Plaster pools often see the pH raise all on its own. That is why plaster pools need acid to lower the pH from time to time but vinyl and fiberglass pools almost never need acid. They will need soda ash often to keep the pH up where it needs to be (7.4 -7.6).

Swimming Pool Maintenance Made Easy

Adding Conditioner

Remember that conditioner has a few names. It is called conditioner, stabilizer, and cyanuric acid.

Tap water has no conditioner in it at all. The recommended range of conditioner in a pool is between 50-80ppm. The conditioner level needs to be tested in the spring and middle of the summer to avoid spending money on chlorine that did not need to be added. Conditioner levels will lower over time if your pool has a leak or if you have a lot of swimmers every summer causing a lot of splash out. Either way, conditioner only lowers from dilution. The normal months to test and add conditioner would be March and July.

Conditioner is sold in powder and granular form. The dosage is the same for both to raise the conditioner levels in your pool. Conditioner is slow dissolving. It may take an entire week for this product to dissolve completely and be part of the pool water. You will add this product (in either form) to the pool skimmer with the pump running. This will put the conditioner directly into your pool filter. The water running through the pool filter every day will help dissolve the conditioner. It helps to have a clean pool filter before this product is added. If you are using the powdered conditioner you will not need to remove the pump basket when adding this product. You simply add the product <u>slowly</u> to the pool skimmer with the pump on. If you add it too fast the product will clump up and become difficult to break up. If you are using the more common granular conditioner you will need to

Swimming Pool Maintenance Made Easy

temporarily remove the pump basket before you add this product. Before you do this make sure there are no leaves in the skimmer that might clog the impeller of the pump when the basket is missing. Then slowly add the product to the skimmer basket using your hand or stirring tool to slowly move the conditioner past the skimmer. If you add it too fast you may cause a clog at your pool pump. You will then need to turn the pump on and off several times causing a surge of water to break up the clog and get the water moving again. Once you have all of the product added put the pump basket back in the pump and turn the system on. Let your pump run for at least 3 hours. Do not clean your pool filter for at least a week or you may lose the conditioner you added if it has not dissolved yet. Cold pool water will add to the time it takes to dissolve.

The amount of conditioner you will need depends on your pool gallonage and the current level of conditioner in your pool. **Add conditioner at the rate of five (5) pounds per 20,000 gallons of pool water in unstabilized or freshly filled pools. This dosage will provide 30 ppm conditioner (cyanuric acid).** You will need to add enough conditioner to reach 50-80 ppm. If you have a salt pool I recommend you only raise your conditioner level to 50 ppm. This is because the salt system is generating new chlorine every day and if the conditioner level is too high you will end up with a very high chlorine level in a very short time.

There is also a liquid conditioner available. This product claims it is better in a few ways. It claims to have a higher pH that will not hurt the pool surface or equipment. It also has the benefit of instant results. The product will start protecting the chlorine

Swimming Pool Maintenance Made Easy

from sunlight the same day it is added. The downside of this product is the cost. On average it is about 3-5 times the cost of regular conditioner. Follow the label on this product for dosage. You will still be adding enough conditioner to reach the 50-80 ppm reading. This product is poured directly into the pool water with the pump on. Let the pump run for a few hours after the product is added to ensure even distribution throughout the pool.

Adding Calcium Hardness

Most tap water has a calcium hardness level of around 50 ppm. The ideal range for calcium in a plaster swimming pool is 200-400 ppm. Test the pool water for calcium hardness to determine the current level of calcium in the pool. It is usually easiest to bring your pool water in an empty water bottle or small container to a pool store for testing.

To raise the calcium hardness level you will need to buy calcium increaser from any pool store. It is sold in granular form. You will add this product at the rate of 1.25 lbs. per 10,000 gallons of pool water to raise 10 ppm. You will put the calcium increaser into a large bucket and add water so that the granular product is completely submerged by several inches of water. Then mix the chemical with a tool or stick. Do not use your hand to mix this product. The water and bucket will get warm or even hot. Pour the mixed product directly into the deep end of the swimming pool <u>slowly</u> with the pump running. It may be necessary to pour some of the mixed product into the pool, stop adding when you see un-dissolved granules in the bucket, and add more water and mix again. Continue to mix with fresh water and add to the deep end until the entire product is added. Run the pool pump for several hours after the product is added to ensure proper distribution.

Removing Phosphates

I have already mentioned that I don't use phosphate removers personally and here is why. Phosphates are naturally occurring and are also introduced many ways. Because of this, for the product to prevent algae, you will need to add the phosphate remover every week. The problems that I have with them is that they are expensive and they clog the filters because of the way that they work. They are sort of sticky, or at least that's the way it ends up when you find it stuck to your filters. They grab onto the phosphates that are in the pool water and hold onto them in the filter until you clean the filter thoroughly. I have had many experiences cleaning a filter from a pool that uses phosphate remover and I can tell you that it is a lot harder to clean the filters. The product is gummy or sticky and it doesn't come off of the filters easily. It also looks like milk and makes a mess wherever you clean the filter. I also feel that phosphate removers shorten the life of cartridge filters.

With that said, some people love phosphate removers and have great results preventing algae using them on a regular basis.

There are take home phosphate test kits available at any swimming pool store. There are too many variations available to mention one style here. Follow the directions that came with the kit and test every month during the spring and weekly during the summer. Keeping a low phosphate level will reduce the amount of algae you might deal with each year. Keeping your filter clean and debris out of the pool in addition to proper number of hours

Swimming Pool Maintenance Made Easy

per day running your filter will also minimize your phosphate levels without a chemical additive.

Phosphate levels should be maintained below 500 ppb.

If you do decide to use a phosphate remover you should have a clean filter and monitor your pressure closely. If the pressure goes up by 8 - 10 lbs. you will need to clean the filter again. Phosphates are always being introduced to the pool so monthly or weekly monitoring would be needed. As mentioned, I personally do not use phosphate removers on the pools I maintain. I think that it should be reserved for pools with continual algae issues with the understanding that the filters will need more attention (cleaning).

With that said, having a high phosphate level in your pool can cause problems with algae (over 500 ppb). You need phosphates, nitrates, and sunlight to create algae in pool water. Nitrates are too difficult to remove and of course we cannot remove the sunlight. Phosphates are easily lowered using any one of several phosphate removers available at most pool stores. Keeping a lower level of phosphates will reduce the number of times you will deal with algae in your pool. Phosphates are constantly being re-introduced to the water so you can never really eliminate them completely. Having a very high level of phosphates in your pool is sort of like having fertilized water. Not all pool water needs a phosphate remover. Have your local pool store test your phosphate level to determine if one is needed. More information was listed above under "Testing Phosphate Levels".

Swimming Pool Maintenance Made Easy

Killing Algae

Identify the type of algae

There are over 400 kinds of algae that can be found in pool water. All of them fit into three major categories (Colors). They are green algae, yellow algae, and black algae.

Killing Green Algae

Green algae are the type of algae you see in the water itself. The water itself has a green color to it. If your water is turning cloudy, chances are you are about to have green algae in your pool. If you have cloudy water, shock your pool with chlorine at the rate of one gallon or one pound granular chlorine per 10,000 gallons of pool water and run the pool pump for up to 24 hours. This may prevent the algae formation.

If the pool has already turned green an algaecide will be needed in addition to the same shock treatment mentioned above. Simply add the chlorine as mentioned and immediately add one quart of "algaecide 60" (60% Poly (oxyethlene (dimethyliminio) ethylene) per 20,000 gallons of pool water. Run the pump for 24 hours and re-test the chlorine level. Add more chlorine and run the pump longer if needed. Make sure the filter pressure stays within range. For example, if the starting clean pressure of your filter is 10 lbs. then you should clean the filter

Swimming Pool Maintenance Made Easy

when it goes up 8-10 lbs. above that. So clean this filter when it hits 18-20 lbs. Brushing the pool may be needed if you notice algae forming on the walls and floor of the pool. Algae that form to the walls grow a protective layer that makes it difficult to kill without brushing it away from the wall. The algaecide used for green algae is "algaecide 60" (60% Poly (oxyethlene (dimethyliminio) ethylene) available at any pool store or online. I have a link to this algaecide at mypoolmadeeasy.com

As mentioned in a section above, sometimes a pool has been green for too long and the steps I just mentioned will not be enough. If you complete the steps above and notice no difference at all one or two days later, you will most likely need to drain the pool and start over. You can rent a submersible pump and pump the green water to a sewer clean-out, wash all of the walls with a high pressure hose and nozzle, fill the pool with fresh water and follow the section in this book called "New pool water start-up". This will save you both time and money.

On the other hand, if you complete the steps above and you are seeing a difference but the algae is still not gone, you can repeat the steps above to further kill the algae. I will say at this point that you can choose to increase the amount of chlorine per 10,000 gallons of water to two gallons liquid chlorine instead of one. Be careful adding too much chlorine because it can bleach out colored plaster and will certainly hurt vinyl pools. I just know that sometimes the extra chlorine is needed to kill very stubborn algae or algae that has a good foothold on the pool because of the length of time it has been there. The high chlorine levels are usually short lived because they will get to work right away on all the algae in the pool. Don't forget the algaecide! You probably won't be successful without it. It does not hurt to add the algaecide more than once (except your wallet).

Killing Mustard Algae

Mustard algae are the most common algae that will still show up in a well maintained swimming pool. The water itself will be clear. The yellow colored algae will form on the walls and in corners or on rocks. It will most likely start on the shady wall first. It brushes off easily like a cloud of dust but will be back in a day or so.

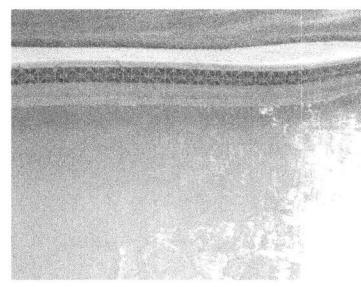

Even if you shock your pool with chlorine and brush the entire pool, without a good algaecide these algae will come back in one to two weeks. The trick with these algae is to be on the lookout for it in the spring and summer months often, and kill it right when you see it.

Brush the pool to remove all mustard algae. Then shock the pool to get the chlorine level over 5 ppm (one gallon of liquid chlorine per 10,000 gallons of pool water). You can then use an algaecide to help kill the algae and prevent it from coming back. I like to start with the same "algaecide 60" mentioned above in the green algae section. That will usually prevent mustard algae from returning. If the mustard algae does return you will need to shock and brush one more time. After this brushing, add a "copper" algaecide to the pool water following the directions on the

Swimming Pool Maintenance Made Easy

"copper" algaecide you buy. This algaecide works very well for mustard algae but should be used only a couple of times per year because you can start to see a copper sulfate stain on white plaster or plastic cleaner parts if used too often. The copper sulfate stain is a turquoise color and is not easily removed. You should never have this problem if you use this algaecide only when the "algaecide 60" is not doing the job. You can also use a sequestering agent to help prevent these stains. See "sequestering agent" below.

Killing Black Algae

Black algae are a small spot (or many small spots) on the walls or bottom of the pool. The spots are not normally bigger than the size of a dime. They grow like a root in the pitted or rough areas of your pool surface, rock areas, or grout. They grow a thick protective head over their root that must be scraped off before killing these algae. A small metal brush is used to scrape the head off exposing the root of the algae to the chlorine and algaecide in the water. First, scrape all black algae in the pool. Second, raise chlorine levels to at least 5 ppm. Then add "black algae killer" or "copper" algaecide to the pool water. Run the pool pump for 24 hours. Follow the directions on the algaecide for dosage. Continue to brush all black algae spots daily for about a week with the stainless steel brush. Having black algae often in your pool might mean you are not keeping the chlorine levels between 1-5 ppm. Black algae will not normally form if there was

Swimming Pool Maintenance Made Easy

enough chlorine in the pool. It is also possible the pool surface is very rough and needs to be resurfaced. Remember to continue to brush the spots until the algae is gone completely. You can also choose to repeat the steps above to further kill the black algae but be careful how much black algae killer or copper algaecide you use over time because too much copper in your pool will likely stain the pool with a copper sulfate (turquoise) color. This stain is difficult to remove. I would say that typically you are fine using a small amount of copper algaecide two times per year without any issues.

Alternative Algaecides

There are mineral purifiers that you can use during the summer season to prevent and kill any of the algae that you might deal with. These products are installed at the beginning of summer and they protect your pool all summer long. Normal algaecides are not added until you have an issue with algae with the exception of maintenance doses.

Mineral purifiers work by using heavy metals such a copper or silver to kill algae and bacteria every day. Minerals kill algae faster than chlorine by at least ten times. They all have similar functions and materials but there are some differences.

All of these systems boast the fact that you can use 50% less chlorine because you now essentially have two sanitizers in your pool.

Here are some of the brands that are available and how they are installed.

Swimming Pool Maintenance Made Easy

Pool Rx - This is a mineral purifier that is easily installed by dropping it into the skimmer or pump basket. This mineral system uses mostly copper to keep the algae away. It also has a sequestering agent in it that will help prevent stains due to the copper. The small plastic device has a dissolvable mineral pack inside as well as a specially treated alloy cylinder. The minerals dissolve and become part of the water. The minerals become disabled when they kill algae and are then rejuvenated when they pass by the alloy cylinder that was installed in one of the baskets. The minerals eventually need to be re-added because they are lost due to filter cleaning, splash out, and evaporation. This system is all in one device and the cost is very low; usually about $100.00.

Frog - The frog system has one model (Instant Frog) that sits in the skimmer basket and uses minerals to kill algae during the summer. The big difference between the Pool Rx and the Frog is that the Frog system uses mostly silver to kill the algae. Silver in my opinion works fine but not as well as copper for killing algae. The big advantage is that silver does not cause any stains in the pool and kills bacteria better than copper. The Frog brand has models that use a canister that is installed into the pool plumbing. A new cartridge is installed every six months or just before summer if you only want to use it during the swim season. The drop in "Instant Frog System" is about $100.00 and treats up to

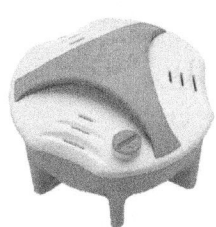

Swimming Pool Maintenance Made Easy

25,000 gallons of water for up to six months. The canister system costs about $270.00 and comes with one six month cartridge.

Nature II – The Nature II brand sanitizer uses a combination of both copper and silver minerals to kill both algae and bacteria. This canister system costs about $200.00 and comes with one six month cartridge. The installation can easily be done by the home owner.

Swimming Pool Maintenance Made Easy

Cleaning Your Filter

Cleaning a Cartridge Filter

Cleaning all brands of cartridge filters is a similar process. Below is a breakdown of the different brands and styles and some of the differences that exist.

The most important part of any filter cleaning is to remember to **turn back any valves** you may have turned before turning the pump back on, and **ALWAYS** open **the air bleed valve** at the top of the filter until water comes out. That will ensure **air does not build up dangerous pressure inside the tank** and cause damage or injury by blowing the top of the filter off and up into the air. Yes, that can happen if you forget to bleed the air when operating your pump after cleaning the filter. There are usually warnings about this on the tank of your filter if the stickers are still visible.

With that said, it really is pretty easy to clean a cartridge filter system. It just takes a little time and effort. Get ready to have your feet get wet! Lol (Welcome to my world)

Pent-air, Hayward, Waterway, or Jandy (4 cartridge filters)

1. To clean a cartridge filter first shut off all pool pumps. Make sure that they will not come back on while the filter is apart. If you are unsure you can shut off the breaker. This extra step might cause you to have to reset the time on your timer.

Swimming Pool Maintenance Made Easy

2. Locate the clamp in the middle of the filter and remove the clamp using a socket set or drill and socket.

3. Open the air bleed valve at the top of the filter.

4. Remove the drain plug at the bottom of the pool filter with a pair of channel lock pliers. Wait a few minutes for the water in the filter to drain out completely and remove the lid of the filter.

5. You will see four filters inside with a plastic spreader holding the filters in place at the top. Pull the plastic spreader off and then remove all four cartridge filters.

6. Clean the four filters thoroughly with a garden hose and spray nozzle. Start at the tops and slowly work your way down each filter. I usually clean about a 3" strip at a time and rotate the filter until complete. This is where you usually get your feet wet. Props if you can avoid it!

7. Clean the o-ring and the grove that the o-ring sits in with water before putting the filter back together. This is important because if you forget and there is sand in that groove or on the o-ring, the filter might not seal and you will have to take it apart again.

8. Clean the inside of the filter tank with water.

Swimming Pool Maintenance Made Easy

9. Clean the little plastic screen that is at the top of the air bleed tube inside the filter. This tube lets some of the trapped air find its way back to the pool during operation. If you are missing the screen on top of the tube you should buy a new one. Small debris can go through this tube back to the pool. This might even clog the next screen inside the wall fitting of your pool cleaner. If this happens your pool cleaner will not work well or at all.

10. Put the filters back and push the plastic spreader back onto the four filters.

11. Put the drain plug back in, the top back on (make sure the o-ring is in place), and tighten the filter clamp with the socket set until the **spring's gaps are closed**.

12. **Leave the air bleed open at the top of the filter.**

13. Make sure you open any valves you may have closed.

14. Turn the filter pump on and wait for all the air to exit the filter. Soon the air coming out of the top of the filter will be water. Shut the air bleed valve.

15. Take note of your new clean starting pressure.

16. Use your weekly maintenance log to record when you cleaned the filter and the starting pressure.

17. Clean the filter again when the pressure rises 8-10 lbs. over this clean starting pressure, or when 6 months have passed, whichever comes first.

Swimming Pool Maintenance Made Easy

Sta Rite Cartridge Filter (System 3)

This filter has 7-8 knobs around the filter instead of a clamp. Inside you will find one tall skinny element and one wide short element. There are arrows on the top of the elements that point in the same direction toward the manifold. Take note of where they are pointing so it will be easier to put them back in after cleaning. The two filters simply pull out and are cleaned inside and out with a garden hose. **The rest of the filter cleaning and bleeding of the air is the same as above.**

Tighten the clamps hand tight only. Sometimes a day or two later, the clamps will need to be retightened by hand when the pump is off because the filter develops a small leak around the middle.

Please read all of the safety information in the 4 cartridge filter section above. **Air build up in a cartridge filter can be very dangerous and should be taken seriously.**

Single Cartridge Filters

Tall skinny filters with one or sometimes two tall skinny elements inside (stacked) are essentially the same as the four cartridge filter except the elements are vertical and there is no manifold at the bottom. There is still a drain plug at the bottom that you will need to take off to drain the water from the tank. There is also an air bleed valve at the top of the lid that you will need to keep open until water comes out after cleaning the filter and turning the pump back on. Please read the 4 cartridge filter section above. The only difference is that most small filters have

Swimming Pool Maintenance Made Easy

different clamp systems that usually do not need any tools. Unfortunately there are many brands and styles that have been made over the years so it is difficult to list them all here. If you are unsure of the correct way to take your small filter apart, search the internet for a video using your filters name. You should be able to find one. If not, feel free to call or email me and I will help you out.

Always open the air bleed valve on top of the filter tank before turning the pump back on after cleaning the filters out. I know I have mentioned this many times but it is probably the most important part because it is the only thing that you can do "wrong", besides not tightening the clamp or lid on the filter or not opening valves that you closed before operating the filter, that could cause injury or even death. Yep, that's right, people have been hit hard enough with the filter top flying off to actually cause death. Please open the air bleed valve at the top of the filter before turning the pump back on after cleaning your filter.

Cleaning a Diatomaceous Earth (D.E) Filter

1. D.E. filters usually have a clamp around the filter that comes off. You can use a socket set or a cordless drill with a socket attachment to remove the nut and spring assembly and that will separate the clamp. Don't loose the two washers that are normally part of that assembly.

2. Most of the time there is a drain plug at the bottom of the filter to make cleaning out the tank easier.

Swimming Pool Maintenance Made Easy

3. Open the air bleed valve at the top of the filter and wait for the water to drain out of the bottom of the filter (drain plug).

4. Remove the clamp and lid. You will see a set of grids held together with a top manifold and bottom spreader covered in a white powder (brown when dirty). The grid assembly does not need to come apart.

5. You can pull the grid assembly out and set it on the ground.

6. Most of the time you will need to pull up and twist back and forth at the same time to be able to pull out the assembly. The top manifold that is part of the assembly will slowly slid off of a 2" PVC pipe that is to one side of the filter.

7. Pick an area of your yard that you can hose off into a drain when done because of the mess this type of filter makes.

8. Use a garden hose to clean in-between and outside of all the grids. Turn the grid assembly upside down and clean from the bottom as well. Turn it back over one more time and clean from the top again. Make sure you try your best to clean in-between all of the grids as much as possible.

9. You can also take the grid assembly apart to clean each grid better but you may have a difficult time learning how to put it back together. Only attempt this if you need to

Swimming Pool Maintenance Made Easy

replace the grids. With the crescent shaped elements, there are 7 full elements and 1 partial. The partial element is not as wide and is positioned where the manifold inlet is to allow for the plastic PVC pipe to connect to the filter manifold.

10. Clean the tank out with the hose including the groove where the big tank O-ring sits.

11. Put the grid assembly back in the tank, sliding the manifold onto the PVC pipe that is to one side, and then put the lid back on. Make sure the top (lid) of the filter is sitting evenly over the thick o-ring and bottom tank. Pick up the large clamp and wrap it around the filter. Insert the bolt part of the clamp through the other side of the clamp and hand thread the spring and nut assembly onto the bolt for at least a few turns. Make sure the two washers are on either side of the spring. If the clamp has a spring (it should) you tighten the nut until the spring rings are touching using a socket set or cordless drill with a socket attachment.

12. Put the drain plug back in at the bottom of the filter.

13. **Make sure the air bleed is still open at the top of the filter and turn the pump back on.** Air will come out of the bleed valve and then water. Shut the bleed valve.

14. The side of the filter will tell you how much D.E. to add back to the filter. Traditionally, if it is a 36 sq. ft. filter you need to add 3.6 lbs. D.E.. Use a 1 lb. coffee can or D.E. scoop to measure the D.E. Add the D.E. powder **slowly to**

Swimming Pool Maintenance Made Easy

the skimmer with the pump on. This will coat the grids with new D.E. powder.

15. **Take care not to breath in the D.E. powder.** Some believe it can cause lung problems or even lung cancer because under a microscope they are like little hooks. If you breathe the dust in, it does not easily leave your lungs. It would be best to wear an N95 dust mask at all times while handling Diatomaceous Earth.

16. Take care to clean the ground where the D.E. filter was cleaned so people can't kick up the dust later and breath it in.

17. Take note of the new filter pressure. This is your clean starting pressure. When the filter rises 8-10 lbs. over this mark, it needs to be cleaned again.

Backwashing a D.E. Filter

Some D.E. filters have a backwash valve on the side of the filter. They are meant to be used in between the complete filter cleaning mentioned above. Some say that the complete filter cleaning above happens once per year and every other month or so, a backwash is all that is needed. I prefer doing a complete filter clean every time the pressure rises 8-10 lbs. above the starting pressure instead. I hardly ever use the backwash valve on a D.E. filter. In my experience it just does not get the filter very clean inside. If you choose to use the backwash valve it is very simple.

1. Turn the pump off.

Swimming Pool Maintenance Made Easy

2. There are two types of valves used. One rotates a handle around to different modes that are labeled on the top of the valve and it's called a Multi Port Valve. You push down on the handle and then rotate it. The other pulls up to backwash and pushes back down for filter mode. This push/pull style valve may have a lock on it to hold it down. Some of the push/pull valves need to have the top handle rotated to unlock the valve in order to pull the handle up.

3. Some D.E. filters have a backwash tank that the D.E. will go through. Inside that tank is a canvas bag. If there is a backwash tank there will also be a gate valve that needs to be opened to allow the water to flow through.

4. When the pump is turned back on, during backwash mode, the water goes through the filter in reverse, knocking most of the D.E. off the grids and washing it out into the canvas bag or onto the ground.

5. If you have the Multi Port valve (Round Valve) you can rotate the handle to "Rinse" and turn the pump back on. Run the pump for a minute to wash out any D.E. that may be trapped inside the system. That D.E. would have returned to the pool without using this feature. Turn off the pump.

Swimming Pool Maintenance Made Easy

6. You can then turn the valve back to "filter" mode and clean out the canvas bag.

7. Shut the gate valve and turn the pump back on.

8. Add 2/3 of the original amount of D.E. that the filter would normally take if it was cleaned all the way (as mentioned above).

9. If there is no backwash tank you will see that the D.E. exited the filter into the yard or next to the filter.

10. Try your best to clean the area that was affected by the backwashing process.

Backwashing a Sand Filter

Sand filters don't need to be taken apart to be cleaned. They all have a backwash valve on them similar to the one on a D.E. filter.

1. Turn the pump off and rotate the valve to backwash.

2. Turn the pump back on and let the pump push the water through the filter in reverse, cleaning the filter sand.

3. The pump can be turned off and on a few times while in backwash mode to try and clean the sand better with surges of water from the pump.

4. If you have a variable speed pump I recommend that you run the pump in the highest speed during the backwash cycle so that you are more successful stirring up the sand and therefore getting a better backwash (cleaning of the sand). Turn the pump off.

Swimming Pool Maintenance Made Easy

5. Rotate the valve back to filter mode and turn pump back on.

6. This type of filter is easy to clean and would be more popular except for the fact that it does not remove a very small particle. Also, the backwashing process does not get all of the dirt out of the filter.

7. After 6 or so years of backwashing the filter the dirt ends up creating channels around the sand and the sand is useless. At that point the sand needs to be removed and new sand added. To try to avoid this, run the pump in the highest speed to backwash better as mentioned above.

There are alternative media that you can put inside a sand filter tank instead of traditional filter sand. Zeolite and Glass are two great alternatives. Both will make the filter pick up a much smaller particle. This means a much cleaner pool with less issues like algae or cloudy water. I only have one Glass filter pool on my route. I have been servicing this pool for almost two years now and it is a very easy pool to maintain. The water is very clear and there have been minimal algae over the last two years. I have to say that I am very impressed by Glass and I need more pools with a Glass filter (a sand filter but with glass inside instead of sand) to fully recommend this type of filter but it sure does look promising. The only reason I won't recommend Zeolite is that you are not supposed to use the 60% algaecide with Zeolite because it degrades it. I love that algaecide too much to give it up. You also only need about half of the Zeolite or Glass compared to sand by weight. Check the manufacture of the product you choose to ensure proper filtration.

Swimming Pool Maintenance Made Easy

Residential pools with sand filters (sand, Zeolite, or Glass) only need to be backwashed once per month unless the filter pressure goes up 8-10 lbs. over the clean starting pressure.

Swimming Pool Maintenance Made Easy

Owning a "Salt Pool"

Thinking about salt? I love salt and the way it feels when you swim but there are a few things you should know before you convert your pool into a salt pool.

Any pool can be a salt pool. The salt system is added to the current pool filtration system by a licensed swimming pool technician. They will add a salt cell to you pool plumbing and install a control board that tells the cell what to do. Next, the proper amount of salt is added to the pool water. Then water runs through the cell when the pool pump is on. Inside the cell is a set of plates and with small amount of electricity (12 volts) electrolysis converts the salt water into chlorinated water.

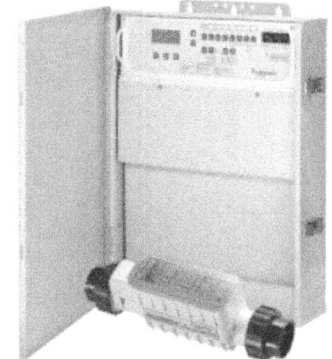

When the chlorine is used up in the pool, it turns back into salt and the process starts over.

Through evaporation and splash out you lose some of the salt every year. In the spring you will need to test the salt level and add the correct amount of salt to the water.

Before changing a current pool to a salt pool there are a couple of things you should consider. The first is the age of the pool surface. If the pool surface is plaster and is already showing signs

Swimming Pool Maintenance Made Easy

of age, adding salt to the water will speed up the deterioration of your pool surface.

A regular plaster pool can be converted to a salt pool but it is likely that the plaster will not last as long as it would have if it were not a salt pool. It is impossible to say for sure but you may loose a few years of life for your plastered pool. Pebble Tech, Pebbly Sheen, Quartz Crystal, or similar "Hard" pool surfaces are ideal for salt because they are not easily damaged from the aggressiveness of salt. The life of these surfaces are not reduced.

The pH will raise quickly requiring muriatic acid from time to time to keep the pH balanced. If you do not test the pH regularly you will ruin the salt cell and possible cause unwanted stains and scale build up to the pool surface. It is not that big of a deal, you just need to know that your pH will change more frequently. Check your pools pH weekly and add the acid that it needs when it needs it.

You will also only want a conditioner level of 50 ppm as a maximum. This is because your system will be making chlorine every day. You will also need to clean the cell every three months. See "cleaning the salt cell" below.

The advantages of having a salt pool is that most people love the way the water feels. Most say the water feels softer and silkier then ever before. It is also true that you will have fewer problems with algae. There is an oxidation process happening when the salt is being changed into chlorine that burns up combined chlorine keeping all chlorine free and ready to work.

Swimming Pool Maintenance Made Easy

That means no chlorine odor and less eye and skin irritation as well as less algae.

Cleaning the "Salt Cell"

The cell is located at the pool equipment and needs to be cleaned every 3 months. Over time the cell will form mineral deposits in-between the plates inside the cell. If left un-cleaned, the cell will have a much shorter life and will not work as well

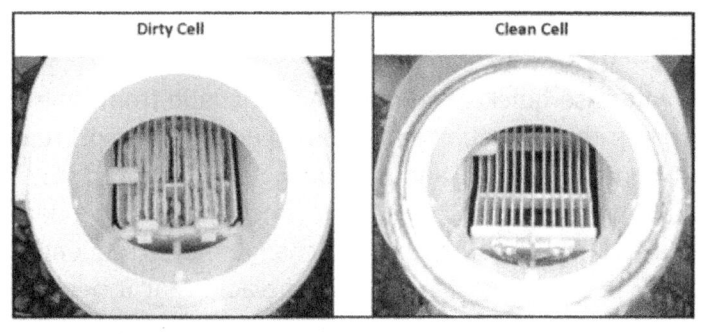

| Dirty Cell | Clean Cell |

including reducing water flow. Most salt cells from different manufacturers are cleaned in the same fashion. It does help to have a cleaning block designed for your cell. You may want to check with the manufacturer of your cell to see if one is available. Muriatic acid is used to breakdown the mineral build up on the plates inside your cell. Rubber gloves will need to be worn at all times when dealing with muriatic acid to prevent burns to your skin. Do not breath the fumes while cleaning the salt cell. Turn the pump off. There are unions on either side of your cell that will unscrew. The cell will then pull out and you can attach it to the cleaning block and stand it up on its end. You can then pour muriatic acid into the cell until the plates inside are covered. You will see bubbling and fizzing inside the cell. This

Swimming Pool Maintenance Made Easy

will last only a few minutes. Once the bubbling stops the acid can be poured into a bucket and the cell can be rinsed inside with water. The cell can then be put back into the plumbing with the unions tightened only hand tight. If you do not have a cleaning block, you can use a bucket. Stand the cell upright in a bucket and pour the muriatic acid into the cell. Be careful not to submerge the outside of the cell in acid. Remove the cell from the bucket and wash with water. In both cases the acid in the bucket should be diluted and neutralized before disposing. You can fill the bucket with more water and then add baking soda to the water to neutralize the acid. You can also add the acid used to clean the cell directly to the pool water if the pH in the pool was on the high side anyway (over 7.6).

If you do a good job keeping the pH in the pool between 7.4 and 7.6 at all times, you will most likely avoid having to clean the salt cell with acid. This is because the cell reverses its polarity automatically every 30 seconds and that along with a lower pH stops the accumulation of salt and calcium from forming on the cell plates in the first place. You should still remove the unions and visually inspect the cell every three months to make sure that it is clean.

Salt cells last from 5-7 years when properly maintained and cost an average of about $800.00 to replace.

Swimming Pool Maintenance Made Easy

Ozonator and their Maintenance

Ozone generators are sold to sanitize your pool water with less chlorine. You will still need chlorine but essentially you will have two sanitizers. The idea is to be able to keep a much lower level of chlorine in your pool and still have clear and healthy water.

Ozone generators are installed in the pools plumbing system (at the equipment pad) and the pool water runs through them. As the water runs through the ozonator, it gets sanitized and then the water returns to the pool. Unfortunately, ozone is not safe for humans so all the ozone needs to be used up before it returns to the pool where it will come into contact with swimmers. Your state or local health regulators might require an ozone detection system as added security.

Ozone is generated by one of two methods: Corona Discharge (CD) or Ultraviolet Light (UV). Both systems use oxygen to create ozone and then transfer the ozone into the pool water using Venturi Injection (a pressure vacuum).

Both types of generators create ozone but in slightly different ways and at different costs.

The CD generator is more expensive to buy but the ozone it creates is a higher concentration and quality. The CD generators require a lot more maintenance. I'm sure that varies depending on the brand but I read a manual for one that one of my customers had and there were several things that needed to be done several times a year.

Swimming Pool Maintenance Made Easy

- Corona cell cleaning to remove contaminates and Nitric Acid
- Clean high voltage terminals
- Replace/rebuild check valves
- Check and test safety components
- Replace Oxygen/Dry Air Feed-Gas Filter
- Check for and repair ozone leaks
- Check and record proper operating parameters

Luckily for me, the customer wants to take care of his CD ozonator himself and I have not seen another one on my route.

The most common type of ozonator is the UV generator and there is less maintenance. Every 6 months the UV light and tube need to be inspected. The tube can be cleaned with diluted muriatic acid or spirit vinegar. The UV bulb is sensitive and should not be touched. It is also very hot and needs 30 minutes to cool down. Please read the manual for the specific brand and model that you own for maintenance instructions for both CD and UV ozonators.

I personally do not sell ozonators to my customers because I can keep their pool clear and healthy without one and they are expensive and need a lot of maintenance. I do realize that there are people that have allergies to chlorine and need a reliable alternative. Ozone can be the right option combined with low doses of chlorine. I have not seen claims that you can use only ozone for proper sanitation.

Swimming Pool Maintenance Made Easy

Using a Flow Meter

A flow meter is a tool used in all commercial pools to tell us how many gallons per minute are passing through the pool equipment. **I like to use flow meters on residential pools as well.** They are installed in the pool plumbing by drilling a hole in the PVC and clamping the flow meter to the pipe. The flow meter has a metal or plastic piece inside that will float when the water goes through it. There are numbers on the front of the meter that tells you the GPM (gallons per minute). GMP is just like Miles Per Hour for your car. If you only knew the RPM in your car you would not know how fast you were going and the same is true for a pool. If we don't know how many gallons are being moved at any one time, we don't know how long to run the filter or what changes are happening when we move valves.

Sometimes a very small valve adjustment will make a big difference in how many gallons of water your pump is moving. You can also easily identify when to clean the pool filter because the flow rate will go down when the filter is dirty. The other reason I like to use these meters on residential pool is because you can now calculate how many hours to run the pool pump. Before the use of this meter you would need to estimate the number of gallons moved in one hour. Now you will know for sure. Just multiply the gallons per minute shown on the meter by 60 minutes. This will give you the gallons per hour. Then divide that

Swimming Pool Maintenance Made Easy

number into the gallons of your pool to tell you the number of hours required by your pool equipment to accomplish one turnover. That is the minimum run time requirement per day for the summer months.

There is also a flow meter that can be added anywhere there is already a check valve in your system. This check valve flow meter is both very accurate and very convenient. Simple unscrew the eight screws on the old check valve and remove the top, replacing it with the flow meter check valve. This flow meter is called FlowVIS by H2Flow Controls.

Variable speed pool pumps need a flow meter even more than a single speed pump. This is because it's not just the valve adjustments that will make a difference in the gallons per minute, the speed of the pump will change this as well. If you use a flow meter, you can raise or lower the speed of your pump and see how much of a difference it makes on the flow. I have found that on every pool if you keep raising the rpm of a variable speed pump, you reach a point where it no longer raises the gallons per minute of the water. At this point there is no point to run the pump that fast. You are not moving any additional water and you would be better off reducing the rpm's of the pump back down where the pump is moving a good amount of water but is not working as hard. This will both save you money and make your pump last longer.

The pump that I install has a flow meter inside it and will display the gallons per minute as well as the rpm's and the watts it is pulling at any speed. This combination of information really lets me adjust the pump to its most efficient speed. Currently

Swimming Pool Maintenance Made Easy

there are two pumps that have these features, the Sta Rite IntelliPro VSF and the Pentair IntelliFlow VSF. Please check mypoolmadeeasy.com for my current recommendations.

Swimming Pool Maintenance Made Easy

Stain Prevention (Sequestering Agent)

Swimming pools will develop certain stains on their surfaces over time. The stains come from poor water chemistry, heavy metals, minerals, or debris (leaves and dirt) that enter pool water over time. To prevent the most common reason the pool surface will stain, simply use this book to maintain proper water balance and try to keep your pool clean all year long.

Unfortunately the pool will probably develop other stains from metals or minerals even with proper chemical balance and great maintenance. These stains are usually light brown or turquoise in color. The only preventatives are a sequestering agent and keeping your pH balanced at all times. You can add a sequestering agent to the pool as much as monthly to prevent stains. Most pools would only need this product **one to two times per year** to offer great stain prevention. A sequestering agent stops the minerals or metals from precipitating out of the water and forming onto the pool surface. It also stops the calcium from doing the same to the pool walls and tile as long as the pH is balanced. This will help the pool walls and tile look new for a lot longer.

Calcium Buildup

Calcium buildup will be talked about separately but I need to mention it here as well. If a pool continually has a high pH, especially when the pool is new or has just been resurfaced, it will build up calcium on the surface and tile. Sometimes this build up will look like it has a different color than the surface of the pool. This is especially true if you have colored plaster like Tahoe blue. Generally speaking the "stains" will be light grey or white and if you feel the walls or tile they will be slightly rough. Unfortunately these are not really stains but instead a chemical reaction caused by poor maintenance. At this point you will most likely need to call an expert. They will drain and acid wash the calcium off of the surfaces or sand it off. This is usually not cheap and should be avoided by doing a chemical startup on all pools if resurfaced or recently filled. Of course, regular pool maintenance should be preformed on all pools at least once per week which will include balancing the pH. A pH kept between 7.4 and 7.6 will stop any calcium build up on your pool surface. You can also use the sequestering agent mentioned above because it works to prevent stains and scale. Sequestering agent will not remove calcium scale that is already built up on your pool surface.

Stain Removal

Ascorbic Acid

Ascorbic Acid is a powdered stain remover. It is actually vitamin C in powder form. Ascorbic Acid sometimes does a great job removing copper (turquoise) or silver (Grey) stains from your pool walls giving your pool a quick makeover. Not all stains are removed by Ascorbic Acid.

You can do a test first before you buy a product to remove stains from the pool surfaces. The test is to take a chewable vitamin C tablet (that you would usually eat), and rub it for several minutes on the pool surface and see if the stain goes away. If it does, you can buy ascorbic acid in powder form from a pool store.

Two pounds treat about 20,000 gallons of water. You would carefully add this powder (it blows away easily) to the pool and run the pump. One hour later brush the entire pool. You might notice a huge difference right away but the stains will continue to go away over a couple of days.

The only downside to this product is that it removes all chlorine from the pool. You will need to wait a week before you slowly raise the chlorine levels back up to normal. If you do this too soon or too fast you may knock the metals that caused the stains back out of the water and onto the walls again. You are also risking causing green algae in the pool due to the lack of chlorine for a week or so. That is why it is best to add this product in the spring when the sun is not as bright and the water is a little more forgiving as far as algae is concerned. If algae does happen, follow the green algae removal section in this book. If you do plan to shock the pool you can dilute the liquid chlorine in a bucket of water first before pouring it into the pool. It is best to only add small amounts of chlorine and then load up the floating chlorinator with tabs to gently raise the chorine level back to a normal.

Oxalic Acid

This product is used to remove brown stains from Iron in the water or stains from dirt or other organic material. This heavy powder should be diluted in a bucket of water and then added directly to the pool water with the pump running. Oxalic Acid will

Swimming Pool Maintenance Made Easy

work slowly over a few days but swimming can continue in about 6 hours. If you want to make the product work even better, you can lower the pH of the pool to 7.0 - 7.2 using Muriatic Acid. Depending on the size of the pool and where the current pH value is, it might need between 1/4 - 1 gallon of acid. Most average size plaster swimming pools would be safe to receive 1/2 gallon Muriatic Acid if the pH was in a normal range before adding the Oxalic Acid. You will need to raise the pH back up to a normal level before you allow people to swim. I would wait 3 days to give the product time to work.

My Favorite Stain Removal Product (Company)

United Chemical makes the two products listed above. Their Ascorbic Acid is called Super Stain Treat and their Oxalic Acid is called Stain Treat. The products work great but the best part is that if you are not having any luck removing the stains from your pool, open a ticket at their website and they will send you free product to help or give you your money back. Who does that anymore? United Chemical does (at least while I am writing this they do). I have a link to the two products at mypoolmadeeasy.com

Alternative Stain Removal

You can also remove stains by paying a pool company to drain and lightly acid wash the walls of you pool. Just know that this process will slightly damage your pool surface by removing a layer of the plaster. If your pool surface is new enough, the reward will easily outweigh the risk.

Swimming Pool Maintenance Made Easy

It may have been bad pool maintenance in the past that caused the stains, and you can prevent that now. After the stains are removed you should start using the sequestering agent mentioned above and take care to always balance the pH and other levels. Also, try to keep leafs and dirt out of the pool as much as possible.

Sometimes turquoise colored stains are not easily removed with any product. These stains are caused by too much copper in the water and a drain and light acid wash might be successful in removing most of the stains. The most common way to fully remove copper sulfate stains (turquoise color) is to resurface the pool. Be careful not to use too much copper algaecide and check to see if the water you are using to fill your pool is already high in copper. Some well water has high levels of certain metals but your water company can offer test results for you to study. If your fill water is the culprit, you should start using a sequestering agent to prevent stains right away, especially if you were successful at removing the stains.

Swimming Pool Maintenance Made Easy

New Pool Startup or Drain & Refill

Whenever you start over with new pool water you will need to balance the water completely. If you have just re-surfaced your pool or if this is a brand new pool you will need to follow these steps. You might also receive directions from your pool resurfacing company and you will probably want to follow those instructions directly because your warranty might require it. It still won't hurt to read this because some of those directions from pool companies don't really explain why each step is needed.

Step 1 - Sequestering Agent

Tap water does not have any ability to prevent staining or calcium build up so a sequestering agent needs to be used. The pump needs to be running and you simply add the required dosage to the pool water directly. There is another product that has evolved some from the standard sequestering agent. This product needs to be added after the pool has been resurfaced and when there is only about 2' of water at the bottom and you are filling the pool. It is called "Startup-Tec" and it will coat the walls of the pool as the pool fills. I now use this product on all of the pools that I am performing a new pool start up on. I have been getting great results. Startup-Tec eliminates 95% or more of the normal brushing associated with new pool startups. It also eliminates the one to two weeks of tedious brushing new pool owners are burdened with. Startup-Tec not only reduces most plaster dust formation, but stops mottling discoloration and staining issues that often plague white, grey, and colored

Swimming Pool Maintenance Made Easy

finishes. The product virtually eliminates acid "hot startups" for all types of aggregate finishes and "acid washing" process necessary to expose pebble type finishes. I have a link at mypoolmadeeasy.com for Startup-Tec.

Step 2 - pH and Alkalinity

Test the pool for pH and total alkalinity. Adjust both to normal levels. If this is a pool that was just surfaced with plaster, exposed aggregate (pebble), or quartz, you will need to **monitor the pH every day.** You will most likely be adding acid in small amounts every day or two to keep the pH at normal levels. Over time (one to two weeks) the alkalinity levels usually end up too low and will need to be raised. After the first month the pH and alkalinity will not change as quickly and you can go back to your normal weekly testing. If you are not sure how to add pH or alkalinity adjusters please read those sections in this book.

Step 3 - Calcium Hardness

Test the pool water for calcium hardness. Most tap water starts out at around 50 ppm (at least where I live). You will need to raise this level to the recommended range of 200 - 400 ppm. I usually try for just 200 ppm. Have the water tested by a swimming pool store because most residential test kits do not include this test. You can ask how much calcium to add if you know the pool gallonage. If you would like the formula it is as follows. 1.25 lbs. per 10,000 gallons of pool water will raise the calcium level by 10 ppm. Examples: If your pool is 10,000 gallons and your new water is only at 50 ppm. you will want to raise the calcium by 150 ppm to get to 200 ppm. To do this you will multiply 1.25 x 15 to get to 18.75 lbs. of calcium needed. If your

Swimming Pool Maintenance Made Easy

pool is 25,000 gallons, multiply 1.25 x 2.5 for a factor of 3.125. Then multiply 3.125 x 15 to get to 46.875 lbs of calcium required. Call or email me if this doesn't make sense. Lol

Adding calcium hardness can be a little dangerous to you and your pool if done incorrectly. Please read the section regarding the correct way to add calcium.

You may also choose to add a smaller amount of calcium hardness compared to the formula above and retest later, adding the extra calcium only if it is needed.

Step 4 - Cyanuric Acid (Conditioner)

You will need to add conditioner to your pool as well. Tap water has no conditioner in it at all. It takes 5 lbs. of conditioner per 20,000 gallons of pool water to raise the conditioner levels by 30 ppm. If you have a 20,000 gallon pool and you want a conditioner level of about 60 ppm you will need to add around 10 lbs. of conditioner. Please read the sections above labeled conditioner.

Step 5 - Chlorine

The last step in the chemical start up is to finally add the first dose of chlorine. It is the least important part and therefore it goes last. In fact, you really don't need the first dose of chlorine until the first week is over. This will give you time to focus on the other levels and it will give the new pool surface time to begin to cure before chlorine is in the water. Simply add 1 gallon of liquid chlorine directly to the pool with the pump running for a 20,000 gallon pool. You will need to retest the chlorine levels with the rest of the other levels often over the next few weeks. That brings me to the next step.

Swimming Pool Maintenance Made Easy

Step 6 - Re-test Everything

When you have new water and especially when you have a new pool or new pool surface, you will need to re-test the pool water for chlorine, pH, alkalinity, calcium hardness, and conditioner every few days to make sure you have added enough of each chemical to reach the desired ranges. This is especially true for the pH and alkalinity levels because with a new pool surface those levels will be changing quickly. I would recommend daily testing and adding small doses of acid or baking soda as needed to balance the water. Don't worry, after a few weeks, the pool surface will have cured some and the big swings for the pH and alkalinity will slow down and you can go back to your normal weekly testing schedule.

If this is a brand new pool or re-plaster, you may want to hire a pool service professional or consult your swimming pool store often to ensure that you balance the pool water correctly. If you do not get it right in the beginning it can mean a damaged pool surface over time. You will also need to follow the directions of your plaster company in regards to brushing the new pool surface for the first two to three weeks. Most pool companies want you to lightly brush the pool two times per day for the first three weeks. Most companies say that you can slow down on the frequency after the dust that you will see starts to diminish. New pool surfaces also require longer run times for you pool filter pump. Most startups require 24 hours per day for the first week and 8 hours per day for the next two weeks. After that you would be able to go back to enough hours to accomplish one turnover per day (typically 4-8 hours).

Swimming Pool Maintenance Made Easy

Always consult and follow the directions of your pool re-surface company.

Swimming Pool Maintenance Made Easy

Re-Surfacing the Pool

In the previous section you will find the directions on the proper startup procedures for your new water. Here I would like to talk about the different pool surfaces available and the approximate costs for each of them.

Pool plaster – This is the most common type of pool surface offered in the past and today. Traditional plaster was white and it is long lasting. The white plaster is smooth and does eventually start to show signs of staining due to contaminates and metals in the pool water. To reduce this effect you should consider adding a sequestering agent two times per year. In recent years the most common color for plaster is "Tahoe Blue". It is actually a grey color but after the pool is full the water reflects the sky to add a dark blue look. Over the years some of the plaster companies have started to add products to the plaster mix that they claim will lengthen the life of the plaster or result in less staining. Some companies have used silicone and others use different types of concrete accelerants. Most of the time I cannot say that these additives help out too much but read the contract to see if a longer warranty is offered because of them. If there is a longer warranty than obviously the plaster company does believe that it

Swimming Pool Maintenance Made Easy

will help. Plaster is still a great and long lasting pool surface today.

I would say that it lasts for up to 20 years but after 15 years you can really tell that the surface is getting older. Most of the issues are cosmetic only like staining and overall discoloration. Eventually the plaster is so thin that you will get what are called "Pop Offs". Pop Offs are like small potholes on a road. The plaster is so thin that the layer of plaster above the gunite lifts off. These areas can be unsightly and even sharp for feet. If you are getting these it is probably time to think about getting quotes for resurfacing your pool.

Regular pool plaster is the least expensive option. The average cost for most pools is between $3,000 and $7,000.

Quartz Plaster - This type of pool surface is supposed to be stronger and longer lasting than typical plaster pool surfaces. The pool surface is still very smooth and comes in many colors. The general look of this surface is exactly like regular plaster. Always ask your re-surfacing company about the longer warranties with this surface to warrant the slightly higher price over plaster.

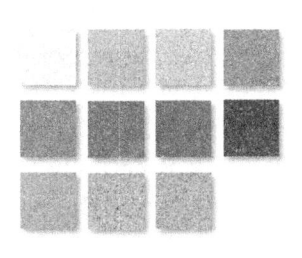

The average price I have seen for quartz is between $5,000 and $9,000 and should last at least 20 years.

Exposed Aggregate (Pebble) - This pool surface has been available for over 30 years but has gained in popularity over the last 15 years. The use of small round and smooth rocks gives the

Swimming Pool Maintenance Made Easy

pool surface a beautiful look. The rocks come in many different colors giving endless options for your favorite look. This pool surface is often referred to as "bulletproof" because it holds up so well to pool chemicals and sunlight. Often this surface looks just as good after 20 years as it does the very first year.

The only downsides to this surface have to do with the space between the small rocks. The rocks themselves are smooth but some complain that their feet are red or sore after an extended stay in the pool. The other issue is that black algae has a little easier time forming between the rocks with this surface type. With that said I have had very few black algae issues with this surface. Usually with proper chemical service you will avoid black algae.

Exposed aggregate is typically more expensive than plaster. The rocks come in different sizes and there are several brand names for each variation that different companies give to their product. The average cost I have seen is between $9,000 and $15,000 and should last at least 30 years.

Fiberglass - This type of pool surface is very smooth and very different than the others available. Some of the differences have to do with the way that the chemical levels behave. A plaster pool will (on average) occasionally need some acid to lower the pH and almost never use "soda ash" to raise the pH. A fiberglass pool will need the pH raised often and should be checked weekly.

Swimming Pool Maintenance Made Easy

Fiberglass can be sprayed over old plaster if you choose this surface. You can also install a fiberglass shell in your yard instead of a traditional pool. Fiberglass is very smooth due to a gel like coating that is applied to the top of the fiberglass to protect it. Fiberglass lasts a long time and has very few downsides. The only issue I have had with fiberglass pools is the gel coat wearing away on the top steps due to use. After the gel coat is gone the surface can easily stain with dirt or other contaminates. This is usually after at least 15 years. I have had a few fibergalss pools that the gel coat is mostly gone and now fiberglass is in the water and no-one uses the pool anymore because they end up itchy every time they do. If it gets to that point you will need to resurface the pool.

The average fiberglass surface costs between $6,000 and $12,000.

Swimming Pool Maintenance Made Easy

Painting your Pool

After your pool is over 10 years old you may notice many stains on the surface caused by metals, minerals, and dirt in the water (make sure you read the stain removal section in this book first). One of the options you have to make the pool look better is to paint it. You will need to drain the pool and prepare the pool surface properly if you plan on the paint lasting a long time and looking good. The pool surface preparation is so important it outweighs every other consideration in this regard.

If you choose to paint your pool you will need to follow the directions that the paint or pool company recommends for best results. Below I will explain what I have learned about pool paint and the process involved.

The idea is to get the pool surface very clean and dry before you put the first coat of paint on the wall. It is very safe to say if you do not do the correct prep work you will see the paint either bubble, peal, or slowly brush off causing many problems for you and your pool filters.

Swimming Pool Maintenance Made Easy

Most paints want you to clean the walls after draining the pool with a three step process. First you should power wash the pool. Second you will use a cleaner similar to the old "TSP" to remove oils and dirt from the surface. Third you will again power wash the walls to remove any of the cleaner before you let the surface dry. Some paints would like you to perform a slight acid wash to the pool surface as well before the last power wash. The last step before you paint the pool would be letting the surface completely dry. Most paints like 3 days to ensure the surface is dry. Then after you paint the pool most paints want another 2 days for the paint to dry before you begin to fill the pool.

As mentioned above, please follow the directions of the paint itself or the pool store and use my input as general information only.

I really should say that I don't personally like this option because I have had customers do this and the paint never seems to last. I have seen the paint fade, chip, peel, and delaminate altogether. Most of those things were probably from incorrect preparations before painting but I just wanted to say that I have never really seen a successfully painted pool that lasted long enough for it to be worth it for me. I know that resurfacing a pool is expensive but it seems to be the only long term solution for an old pool.

Empty pool precautions

There are some considerations you should think about before draining your pool for any length of time. The season you are in

Swimming Pool Maintenance Made Easy

will make the biggest difference. Think of your empty pool as a boat. If the ground water is too high around your pool on the outside it can literally float your pool up a few inches. This will cause severe damage to your pool that you may not be able to fix. It is possible to cause cracks in the pool walls or bottom as well as other foundational issues. If you are planning to drain your pool during or directly after the rain season you should consult an expert to perform this task.

If you are thinking about having your pool re-surfaced, you do not have to rule out having it done during or directly after the rain season. If the plaster company is concerned about this issue they will drill several large holes in the bottom of the pool allowing water come up through the bottom of the pool which will relieve pressure. The holes are easily filled the day they re-surface the pool and start filling it back up. You may also find that the plaster companies are very accommodating this time of year because they receive so little business. You may also see a lower bill with more time spent on your job specifically. If rain or bad weather is in the forecast, delays are certain.

Some pools are equipped with a device in the main drain called a hydrostatic valve. The hydrostatic valve is like a check valve. It only allows water to flow one direction. In this case it will not let the pool water flow out of the pool when the pool has water in it but it will let ground water to flow into the pool when the pool is empty. You will not know if your pool is equipped with a hydrostatic valve unless you have the plans to the pool or if a professional tells you you do.

I would not recommend draining in or directly after the rain season if it can be avoided at all. If you are going to drain the pool for a reason such as a very green pool, you should plan on refilling the pool right away. This will minimize the risk. You can also call your water company and ask for your current water table readings. This might help you figure out how high the water is in the ground around your pool before you drain.

Swimming Pool Maintenance Made Easy

Choosing the Right Pool Equipment

This section will help you look at the equipment you currently have and make a decision about how effective and energy efficient it all is. There are several ways that changing one or more pieces of pool equipment will give you a much easier to maintain pool, or a much more energy efficient one. Sometimes it is smartest to wait until you are having problems with a pump or need new parts for a filter before you act. Too many times I have seen people put a lot of money into old pool equipment that should be replaced. Some older pool equipment is essentially the same as the new version and you will not benefit by replacing it before it fails. I will do my best to help you decide.

Pool Filter

Changing the filter will probable make the biggest difference for your swimming pool. This could be a bigger difference than any other piece of equipment. The right pool filter makes the biggest difference in two areas; efficiency and effectiveness.

The first is how many gallons per minute that old filter will allow to go through it at one time (flow Rate). The filter most likely has a sticker on the side of it that will give you this number. A low flow rate is any number under 100 gallons per minute (GPM). Most D.E. filters have a very low flow rate (less than 75 GPM). Most small cartridge filters also have a low flow rate (less than 100 GPM). Having a low flow rate and a powerful pump will just result in a lot of back-pressure (high pressure reading on top of the filter) but no additional water movement. A smaller

Swimming Pool Maintenance Made Easy

horsepower pump would have moved the same gallons per minute with less back-pressure on the pump so the bigger pump did you no good. If you change the filter out to a large cartridge filter (with a flow rate of over 125 GPM), you will move more water per hour and therefore need to run the pump less per day to accomplish the same thing (saving lots of money). Even the newest D.E. filters still have low flow rates. Almost every cartridge filter over 300 Sq. Ft. has a flow rate of 125 GPM or 150 GPM. Sand filters also have very low flow rates and if you use regular sand you will not be able to keep your pool water as clean as the other two types. There is however, alternative media that you can use inside a sand filter other than sand. Glass will help you keep the water very clean and you only need half the weight compared to sand to do the job. Even with all of that said, glass media in a sand filter still has a low flow rate.

The second big difference is how clean the water will get and how much debris/dirt the filter will hold before it needs to be cleaned. A D.E. filter is sold in 24,36,48,60, and 72 sq. ft. sizes. To compare a D.E. filter to a cartridge filter for square footage, you need to double the D.E. size. Example: If you have a 60 sq. ft. D.E. filter, double that when comparing it to a 300 sq. ft. cartridge filter. That would be 120 sq. ft. compared to 300 sq. ft. Even the largest D.E. filter is smaller than the smallest cartridge filter made today. A 300 sq. ft. cartridge filter will hold up to 15 lbs. of dirt/debris. You only need to clean a large cartridge filter every 4-6 months. Cartridge filters work by clarification. That means they only pick up large particles when they are recently cleaned. They allow the smaller particles to go right through the filter. Then the next time the water goes through the filter it will

Swimming Pool Maintenance Made Easy

pick up a little smaller particle. Eventually (6-7 pass-troughs) the filter will be picking up particles almost as small as a D.E. filter will. The best part is the dirt/debris is helping the filter trap smaller particles. That is why they have been making cartridge filters so big in the last 10 years. Because cleaning a small cartridge filter more often is just a bad idea. When you select a cartridge filter, choose the next size up from the one needed for your pool. You will not need to clean it as often and the cartridges inside will last longer. There is usually only a small difference in price between the two sizes. The brand of the filter makes a small difference. The simple idea of "you get what you pay for" applies. The more expensive filters are usually made with thicker and better materials that should last longer. With that said, the difference is small and may not make a big enough difference when you consider saving 30% or so. This depends on your budget and individual personality. Changing out the pool filter can save you as much as 50% of your energy usage if you have an old inefficient pool filter.

Pool Pump

The pool filtration pump is the piece of equipment responsible for moving water from the pool through the pool filter and other equipment, and then back to the pool. There have been many attempts over the years to make these pumps move more water and cost less per hour to run. Some of the advances have made a huge difference (Variable Speed Pumps) and some not so much (Two Speed Pumps).

As a side note, here in California, we are not allowed to install a single speed pool pump for filtration. We can only install a two speed or variable speed pump. There is one exception, if the single speed pump has a total horsepower of under 1 HP. I am actually happy about this regulation because the variable speed pumps do so much more than a single speed pump, they are also very quiet, and they save a ton of money in energy costs. I have tested many pump replacements and on average a variable speed pump saves pool owners about 70% over a single speed pump. By the way, I don't believe two speed pumps save us any money. I really think variable speed pumps are the way to go. With that said, I will still try to explain all pump options. You may live in a state that still allows single speed pumps. They are cheaper to replace and that might be the only reason to install one.

Single Speed Pump

A single speed pump can be energy efficient and move a lot of water if sized correctly but even the most efficient single speed pump will not be nearly as efficient as a **variable speed pump**. Single speed pumps run at the same speed all the time and pull the same amount of energy (amps) when running. If your pump is over 15 years old you should consider replacing it. There have been enough changes in that time that you will benefit greatly. How efficient your single speed pump is depends on its size (horse power), size of pool plumbing, distance from pool, and other equipment involved. Some of the pumps were not sized correctly from the beginning. Years ago people thought bigger is always better. With pool pumps this is simply not true. You do need a big enough pump to get the correct amount of water to each water feature you have. This is where having a professional come out to your house and look at everything involved

Swimming Pool Maintenance Made Easy

sometimes helps. Here are some of the things the professional will look for.

Plumbing size

The plumbing size used for your pool makes a big difference on what size pool pump you can install and how efficient your pool can be. You may have copper or PVC plumbing coming from the ground at your pool equipment pad. The size of the plumbing also varies. If you have copper plumbing the size can range from 1", 1.25", 1.5", or 2". The smaller the plumbing, the smaller pump you will have to go with (single speed). This is because you can only force a certain amount of water through a certain size pipe. Copper pipe has the disadvantage of thinning over the years (especially if the pH was not maintained) so you do not want a pump too powerful because you may cause leaks. Using a smaller pump and running it more hours per day is the smarter option here. Also, a variable speed pump mentioned below can be programmed to run at a slower speed for smaller pipes or older copper plumbing. PVC plumbing is the most common. It is most often found in 1.5" and 2". Sometimes you will see 2" plumbing coming from the ground and then it is converted down to 1.5" to go into the pump or somewhere else at the equipment pad. This is where you have a big opportunity to change the pump and use the 2" pipe all the way to the pump and through the rest of the equipment as well. Then you will choose the best horse power and start moving more water than you ever did before. This will save you money because you will not need to run the pump as many hours per day to accomplish the one turnover per day required.

Swimming Pool Maintenance Made Easy

Horse Power of Pump

The horse power of the current pump will need to be evaluated. Below are the factors involved. Variable Speed Pumps are adjusted differently. More on that later.

Distance from Pool

The distance from the pool to the pool equipment and back is measured as "feet in head". A technical term used to help determine the size of pump needed for your pool. If your pool equipment is 50' away from your pool and 7' higher than the pool water, you will need a bigger and more powerful pump to move the same amount of water as a smaller pump would move if those factors were not there. Most pool equipment is within 20' of the pool and at or just above ground level. When this is true you will not need to worry about this factor. If your equipment is far away and higher than the pool, I hope you have large plumbing because if you don't you will have a very hard time getting enough water to go to the pump. This will cause your pump to pull more energy (amps) and move less water. It may also cause your pump to cavitate. That means your pump is too big and it is trying so hard to pull water from the pool but it just can't pull enough. It will make a noise similar to having marbles bumping around in the pump and the motor on the pump will be loud and hot. Your pump will not last as long. Relocating the pool equipment would be expensive but might be your best option. The other option is to downsize the pump to a variable speed pump and minimize the amount of water it can move. You will then need to run your pump more hours to accomplish one turnover per day.

Swimming Pool Maintenance Made Easy

Size and Type of Filter

When we talk about the size of the filter in regards to the pool pump, we are really only looking at the gallons per minute rating on your current filter or proposed new filter. The type of filter is needed for the same reason. We just need to know how many gallons of water your filter can handle per minute because the pumps are rated at how many gallons they move. If you go online you can find a pump curve chart for almost every pump out there. This chart will use the distance the equipment is from the pool x 2(feet in head), and the horse power of the pump to tell you how many gallons it should be moving. You will need to make sure your pump is not trying to move more water than your filter can handle.

Other Water Features Involved

Having other water features with your pool will make a difference in your pump selection as well. You may have a spa attached to your pool. You will not want to go with too small of a pump here unless you have a dedicated pump just for the spa jets. Otherwise you may not have the desired effect when using the spa. If you have solar on the roof of your house you will want to count the number of panels. Most solar panels will only handle about 5 GPM each. That means if you have 8 panels you can only force 40 GPM through the solar during the time the solar is on. If you have a pump that is too powerful and there is no bi-pass line installed allowing extra water to go around the solar, you will simply have a very high pressure on your filter (entire equipment) which is just back-pressure. You will still only be moving 40 GPM when the solar is on. This is not good for the solar, pump, filter,

Swimming Pool Maintenance Made Easy

plumbing, or any other piece of equipment installed. This is one of the reasons a variable speed pump can be beneficial. Certain automatic pool cleaners also need to be considered. There are some cleaners that will not work well if the pump is too small. The rule of thumb is, if your pool has a pressure side pool cleaner without a booster pump the smallest pump you should install would be a 1 hp. If you have a suction side pool cleaner you will get better results with a 1 hp. pump as well. If you have a booster pump you do not need to worry about the filter pump size because it takes small amounts of water from the filter pump and puts it under a lot of pressure making the cleaner move. Any size pump above ½ hp. will be fine.

Two Speed Pumps

About 20 years ago the two speed motor was created and used for swimming pools. They were promoted as energy efficient motors. The idea was that you would run the pump in the low speed most of the time and the high speed for only a couple hours per day. The high speed would be needed to run your pool cleaner or other water feature that needed more water movement. The problem with these pumps that many people do not realize is that if you compare the number of gallons moved per day compared to a single speed pump, and do the math on how much each one costs to accomplish the same thing, the two speed pump costs more. That is because the low speed moves very little water but still pulls a good amount of energy (amps). It does pull

Swimming Pool Maintenance Made Easy

fewer amps than it does in high speed but the math is just not there.

Example: If your two speed pump pulls 3.5 amps in low speed and moves only 20 GMP, and pulls 6.5 amps in high speed but moves 65 GPM. You will need to calculate how many hours per day you need to run the pump in each speed to accomplish one turnover. If your pool is 20,000 gallons and you decide to run your high speed only 2 hours per day, you will need to run the low speed 10 hours per day (2 hours @ 65 GPM = 7,800 gallons, 10 hours @ 20 GPM = 12,000 gallons). Let's say you are spending $.20 per kilowatt hour, it would cost you $.62 for the high speed and $1.68 for the low speed = $2.30 per day to move 20,000 gallons of water. Compare that to a single speed pump that pulls 6.5 amps per hour and moves 65 GPM. That pump will only need to run 5.13 hours per day. At the same $.20 per kilowatt hour, this pump will cost you $1.60 per day to move 20,000 gallons of water. This means you will save $.70 per day or $21.00 per month with the single speed pump running the correct number of hours per day.

There has been recent development attempting to make the low speed more efficient. Time will tell.

Variable Speed Pumps

These pumps should be on all swimming pools old and new. They are very energy efficient and also quiet. There really isn't a good reason to use a single speed or two speed pump as your main filtration pump anymore because this style pump beats the other pumps across the spectrum. Here is why.

Swimming Pool Maintenance Made Easy

Variable speed pumps can be programmed to run at different speeds when different pieces of equipment are on. For instance, if you are running the solar you can slow the pool pump down to accomplish the 40 GPM mentioned above, but when the solar is off and the spa is on you can speed up the pump to get the desired results in the spa. You will need a timer system designed for this pump if you also want valves to change with the pumps changing speeds. Otherwise the pump can be programmed to change speeds for simple tasks that do not require valve movement like a higher speed for 2 hours while the pool cleaner runs and a low speed for the rest of the time for normal filtration. Variable speed pumps are on all new swimming pools. They can be used for all water features and are especially helpful when different speeds are needed for different tasks. The motor on this pump uses permanent magnets instead of copper windings like all other pool motors and runs on direct current (DC) instead of alternating current (AC). This gives the new motor a couple of advantages. The first is the ability to run the pump in many different speeds using the attached controller or pre-programmed speeds on the pump. The second is the fact that this motor does not get as hot. Heat can cause damage to the bearings of a standard motor. The third advantage is how quiet these motors can be. In the lower speeds it is sometimes difficult to tell if the pump is even running. The last advantage is the cost savings. That is what needs to be addressed the most.

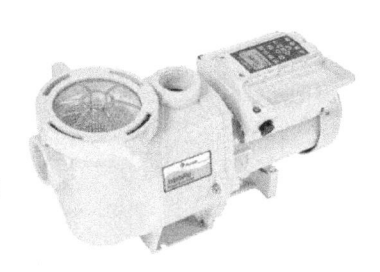

Swimming Pool Maintenance Made Easy

The cost savings of a variable speed pump depends on the speed you choose to run the pump in and the number of hours per day it runs. A flow meter on the plumbing would help you calculate the correct number of hours required to complete one turnover per day (see "using a flow meter" for more info). Otherwise you may run the pool too much or not enough. Most of these pumps show you how many watts they are using at the current speed which is very helpful.

My favorite variable speed pump will tell you the GPM (Gallons per minute) as well as the Watts they are pulling. These are the Pentair Intelliflo VSF pump and the Sta Rite Intellipro VSF pump (owned by Pentair). They are so quiet my customers love them for that reason alone. I love them because you can fine tune them to be the most efficient and effective using the sensors that they come with. I will raise the RPM of the pump while watching the GPM and Watts pulled change. As I raise the RPM eventually the GPM stops going up. This is because I have reached the limits of this pools plumbing. I usually slow the pump down a few hundred RPM's from there and make sure the water is moving well to the pool cleaner and skimmers. If all of that works well then I have found the speed that I will use to run the pool. Every pool is different because of plumbing sizes and so on, but with this pump I can really make everything work the way it should and be as energy saving as possible.

Pool Heater

Gas pool heaters that are under 20 years old all have a bi-pass line inside. That means they will not slow down the water very much that goes through them. The only exception is if the heater

Swimming Pool Maintenance Made Easy

is old enough to use small copper plumbing. This plumbing may be a lot smaller than the rest of the plumbing at the pool equipment. If you change out the heater with a new heater, you will be able to use the larger pipe that the rest of your equipment uses. Otherwise, if you are considering replacing the heater it would be for its cost savings to operate. They give an efficiency rating to all heaters. The very old heaters were at about 72% efficient. That meant that 72% of the heat generated was available to heat the water. New heaters are at about 84%. This combined with the fact that heaters loose some of their efficiency over time; you can save a lot of money. I still like to wait until the heater needs a repair before replacing it. Most heaters with installation cost about $3000 plus tax. If you use your heater a lot it might be worth it.

Caretaker System (Pop Up Jets)

Some pools have their return lines on the sides of the pool with eyeball fittings to direct the water and some have pop up jets at the bottom of the pool. The pop up jets sometimes rotate every time they come on and they all slowly switch between two or three jets at a time going around the pool. The idea is that one or two jets will push the dirt and leafs to the next set of jets until it reaches the bottom suction where it is removed (to the filter).

Caretaker is a brand name of one of these systems that was very popular for many years so now a lot of poop people will just say that you have a caretaker system when it might actually be made by a different company.

Swimming pools with pop up jet systems usually do not have automatic pool cleaners such as a Polaris because they are not supposed to be necessary. To that I would say, if the system is designed well and the jets are placed in the right location, you might not need a pool cleaner. Unfortunately, if the system does not end up working well you might have very few options to supplement. This is because the pool builder usually does not give you a dedicated plumbing line and fitting to connect a pool cleaner. This usually means that if you do want an additional pool cleaner you will need to buy a robotic pool cleaner.

Robotic Pool Cleaners

Swimming Pool Maintenance Made Easy

Robotic pool cleaners are pretty cool and some pools can't use a regular pool cleaner. They use very little energy (pennies per day) and they do a decent job cleaning the pool and not getting stuck. They range in price from around $600 - $2,500 depending on several features and intended purpose. The real expensive ones are used in commercial pools like apartment complexes and water parks/hotels. Some of the cleaners come with a caddy to move the unit around when it is not in the pool.

All of the robotic cleaners that I have seen recently have a controller that lets you set a timer for 1,2, or 3 hours of run time. Some can be controlled by your phone. Most manufactures do not expect you to leave the cleaner in the water at all times like a Polaris pool cleaner. They expect that you will only be putting the cleaner in the pool when the pool needs to be cleaned. With that said, I have several customers that leave the cleaner in at all times and they seem fine so far. I do have one where the cord looks like it is wearing from the chemicals so I would say it's probably best to keep them out unless in use.

As far as which unit to buy, they are always changing so it's hard to say. I will say that I really don't like the ones with bags inside to clean and if I was going to buy one it would have a filter or container to catch the material so it is easier to clean. Polaris now has a robotic pool cleaner and it works well. Maytronics has many cleaners and they have been around forever. There are several more brands and I'm sure there will be new companies making them in the future. Check reviews and do your research to find the best one for your pool. Good luck!

Swimming Pool Maintenance Made Easy

In-Ground Pre Filter

If your pool has pop up jets it is likely to have a pre filter basket in the ground with a lid on it. Basically, the suction drain at the bottom of the pool pulls a lot of leaves into it and then those leaves would be too numerous to go straight to the pump basket so the pool builder might install one of these. You will see a clear lid that comes off with a quarter turn and inside is a very tall basket. You will need to clean this basket along with the rest of your maintenance and cleaning items weekly. Make sure you turn off the pump before opening the lid or your pump will suck in air and loose its prime. Also, don't loose the o-ring under the lid when you remove it. Keep the o-ring clean to insure a proper seal.

Swimming Pool Maintenance Made Easy

Pool Has a Leak!

What do you do when you think your pool might have a leak? The first thing you should do is to verify that you do actually have a leak. The method I recommend is the simple "Bucket Test".

The Bucket Test

Take a bucket and set it on the top step of the pool. Fill it higher than the pool water level so the bucket will stay put. You can mark the bucket with a marker or tape at it's current water level. Fill the pool to a specific line as well. The bucket does need to be exposed to the same elements as the pool including sunlight and wind because both will evaporate water. The reason I recommend putting the bucket on the top step of the pool is so the two water temperatures are the same as well. Wait three days to a week to go by without filling either the bucket or the pool. If the pool water goes down by more than the bucket, then you have a leak by that amount.

Example: If the bucket goes down by one inch and the pool went down by two inches, you have a one inch per week, leak in your pool.

You can do some more tests before you hire help to find and fix the leak that will be helpful to that person. Start over with the bucket test and this time don't run the pool equipment at all for three days. Measure the results. Start over again with the pool equipment running 8 hours per day and measure the results

Swimming Pool Maintenance Made Easy

again. This might help point in a certain direction as far as where your leak might be.

After you have determined that you do have a leak in your pool you can try to find it and fix it yourself before you hire a professional. Most pool leaks are found in the skimmer. There is sometimes a crack or separation that develops between the plastic skimmer and the concrete pool. Inside the opening of the skimmer you will find pool tile that stops at the skimmer. Look for a crack or separation at this spot. If you cannot see a crack you can use a dye to help out. If you have a test kit you can use the pH test solution. Without moving the water, and with all pumps off, carefully squeeze the dye near the separation mentioned above. Do not move your hand and watch the dye to see if it is pulled into the crack. If it is, you can purchase a grout repair compound called "dry lock" from a home improvement store. There may also be a product available at your local pool store and you can also use an epoxy putty. You would follow the label instructions on whatever product you purchased and attempt to fill in the crack or separation as much as possible. Do the bucket test one more time. If the leak is not fixed it is probably best to call a leak detection company. They will find and fix your leak. The companies I have near me charge about $300 to do their tests and then more to fix the issue.

Leak Detection Companies

Most cities have several leak detection companies to choose from. Leak companies will do the dye test mentioned above but they also have many other tricks up their sleeves. They will take apart valves and plug lines to apply pressure on each pool return

Swimming Pool Maintenance Made Easy

separately. They will look for a loss of pressure on each line and if they find one they have sound equipment that will pinpoint exactly where the leak is underground so that the least amount of work is needed. They have ways to test pool lights and spa jets. Long story short, if you can't find your leak, hire a leak detection company. It should end up being money well spent.

A Long Term Leak Can Cause Permanent Problems

Even a small pool leak can cause permanent problems because dirt is usually eroded over time causing pool settling and even cracks in the pool for the worst cases. Erosion will also cause the pool deck to shift and sink creating ugly concrete and tripping hazards. If you think your pool has a leak, it is best to fix it as soon as possible to avoid theses issues.

Swimming Pool Maintenance Made Easy

Pump Lost its Prime - What Now

If your pump was running fine and then all of a sudden it won't move water, here are some common things to check before you call an expert.

Check the water level of the pool. If the water level is close to the bottom of the tile this might be the reason. The pool pumps pull water from the top of the pool first and if you don't have enough water in the pool to fill the skimmer and keep it full as the pump runs, the pump will pull in air as it runs until it looses its prime completely. If this has happened you should shut off the pump right away and fill the pool. The pump might self prime after the pool is full but there are some things that you should do to remove the air that it pulled in. Remove the pump lid and fill the basket area with water. Put the lid back on and turn on the pump. Bleed the air from the top of the filter using the air bleed valve. After water is flowing through the pump and all the air is out of the filter, look for leaks around the pump. If the pump ran for too long you may have a bad shaft seal in the pump behind the impeller. You will know if you do if water continues to accumulate every time you run the pump. You will need to replace the shaft seal.

If the water level in your pool is halfway up the tile line (the most common place it should be) then check the skimmer weir to see if it is getting stuck. The skimmer weir is the plastic gate or door that is inside the opening of the skimmer between the basket and lid area and the pool itself. You can reach inside the

Swimming Pool Maintenance Made Easy

skimmer (where the basket is) and feel the weir. They hinge from the bottom and move back and forth as the pump turn on and off. The idea is that when the pump is on they allow water and debris to enter the skimmer but when the pump shuts off they float up to the closed (upright) position to keep the debris in the skimmer area. Sometimes they get stuck because a stick or other item gets to the side of the weir in between the pool wall and the weir. Then the weir will not move and not enough water is able to flow to the pool pump. Eventually air fills the plumbing lines and the pump looses its prime. Free up the weir and follow the directions above to get the water moving again. Some of the weirs are aftermarket and they only stay in because they have a spring and rubber pads that push against both sides of the skimmer. The weir then hinges from this area (at the bottom) and works as described above. Sometimes people jumping into the pool (cannonballs) push too much water into the skimmer at once and move the weir out of place. Once the weir is a little sideways it is likely to get stuck. The weir can easily be moved back into place by pushing it down and then against the ledge at the bottom of the skimmer where it is supposed to be. Move the weir back and forth to ensure that it moves and does not get stuck and then follow the re-priming

Skimmer With Equalizer

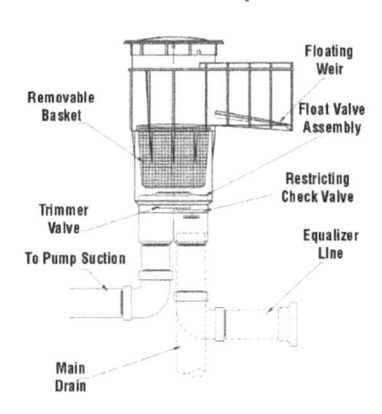

Swimming Pool Maintenance Made Easy

instructions to the pump mentioned above. Ask all swimmers to refrain from cannonballs or check the weir often.

Another reason you might loose the prime of your pump is if there is an obstruction in the line. Were you recently vacuuming the pool? Did you run the pump without baskets or with damaged baskets where debris could have gotten through and clogged the impeller of the pump? If any of those are true you can try to flush out the line or clean the impeller.

If it is the line that you think is the problem, try using a drain jet to loosen the debris. A drain jet is a tool that you put on the end of a garden hose and it expands to the size of the pipe while also pushing water out the end. This will seal the plumbing at one end and create pressure in the pipe to clear the clog. You may have to try it in both directions to get the water moving again. Try (with all equipment off) putting the drain jet inside the pump (remove the pump lid first) towards the plumbing on the suction side of the pump. Turn the water pressure on all the way and go over to the pool skimmer. Remove the skimmer basket and float valve under the basket. Look for debris to be coming out of the holes at the bottom of the skimmer. You can also start at the skimmer and push the water towards the pump. There are usually two holes at the bottom of the skimmer. The one that is furthest from the pool is the one that goes to the pump. The other is the one that goes to the bottom drain in your pool.

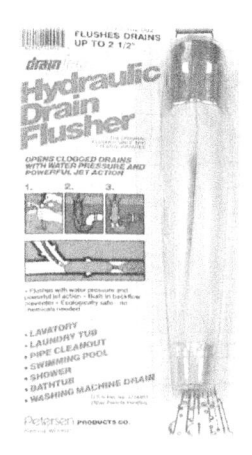

Swimming Pool Maintenance Made Easy

Put the drain jet in the hole furthest from the pool and turn the water on all the way. Remove the pump lid and let the water overflow there. Look for debris to see if you are making any progress. If you are sure there is a clog you can go back and forth between these two spots and you will eventually loosen the debris. Put the pump basket back on and put the skimmer back together. Turn the pump on and see if it primes. If it won't you may need to call a pool person that can use compressed air instead of a drain jet.

The last reasons your pump won't prime is if the impeller is clogged or if there are leaks in the pool plumbing where air is being pulled in and not enough water is able to be pulled. Both of these reasons and solutions should probably be solved by a professional. If you have tried all of the above to no avail feel free to email or call me. I might have a different solution after hearing what was going on after the last time the pool was running properly.

Swimming Pool Maintenance Made Easy

Leaks at the Pool Equipment

There are many different places your pool equipment can leak. Most are on the pressure side which means you will see the leak as the pump runs. The other possibility is that you have a leak on the suction side of the pump. In this case air will be entering the pumps it runs and subsequently filling the filter tank with air as well. You should also see air bubbles returning to the pool as the pump runs if this is true.

If you are getting air entering into the pump as it runs it can be difficult to find the source. Leaks can happen at any fitting or valve as well as right at the pump where the plumbing enters. If the pump ever ran dry and therefore got hot, you mot likely have a leak at the fitting that enters the pump on the suction side. This is because the heat can slightly melt or warp the threaded fitting and air will be able to get around the treads. If you have unions in front and on top of the pump you can try replacing the o-ring in both locations to try to stop the leak. One way to find the leak on the suction side of your equipment is to use a drain jet with the pool equipment off. In the previous section I talk about the drain jet and how to put it in the second hole from the pool inside the skimmer. That is what you need to do again but this time do not remove the pump lid. The water will be heading towards the pump and it will continue through the pump and filter and then go back to the pool. Because it is going through all of that equipment a little bit of back pressure will occur. This means that wherever the leak is, you should see water coming

Swimming Pool Maintenance Made Easy

out, even if it's on the suction side. Once you see the leak you can figure out what will be needed to fix it.

PVC leaks can be resolved by re-plumbing that section. Make sure you use good PVC glue like "Pool Tite" or "Red Hot". PVC "Glue" is not actually a glue but a solvent. The PVC is actually melted to the other PVC and these two products do not give you very much time to move fittings around so make sure you are ready to go before you push the fittings onto the pipe. No primer is needed with these products. You need to sand off any PVC paint before gluing new fittings to the old PVC.

Pumps have a few areas that can leak. You can run your dry hand under some of these locations and check for moisture. The two easiest spots to fix if they are leaking is the two drain plugs. On one side of the pump you will find two small finger knobs that can be removed to winterize the pump in freezing areas during the winter. Those drain plugs have small o-rings on them that get old and crack. The o-rings are inexpensive and easy to replace.

The pump might also be leaking at its shaft seal which is behind the impeller inside the pump. This would be common on a pump that ran dry (without enough water) for any amount of time. The shaft seal can be replaced easily if you know how but it might be a job for a pool professional if you are not super handy. There are You Tube videos on almost every pump that should walk you through it if you would like to attempt it yourself. The shaft seal is inexpensive ($15 - $30) and you can download the manual for your pump to see which one you need. Most pool professionals charge between $150 - $250 to do it for you. Before you pay this money or do all that work yourself, try to make sure that is

Swimming Pool Maintenance Made Easy

where the water is coming from. Use your dry hand and put it under the pump where the motor meets the plastic pump volute. Do not stick your fingers up into the running motor but simply feel for moisture right by the motor. Chances are if you feel any water, your leak is at the shaft seal. If it is dry, check the area right next to that spot where the two plastic pump parts separate. Most pumps have a stainless steel clamp or bolts at this spot. There is a simple o-ring or shaped rubber seal that can easily be replaced to stop your leak. If you take your pump apart for any reason you will need to fill the pump with water before you turn it on again. The pump will not prime on its own without water in the pump to start.

Filters can also leak at the unions which is where the PVC pipes connect to the filter. The unions can be unscrewed and the o-rings can be replaced to stop the leak. Certain union leaks on some filters require you to take the filter apart because there is a second o-ring on the union that pushes up against the filter tank itself. It might be easier to hire someone for this one because sometimes the plastic parts break and need to be replaced.

You can take a picture of your leak and email it to me. I will try and give you advice if I can.

Swimming Pool Maintenance Made Easy

Shade Cover for Pool Equipment

I am adding this topic to the book because I have seen how much longer pool equipment lasts if it is protected from the sun. Most of the pool equipment is made of fiberglass reinforced plastic. It is not like the pool equipment of the past that was made from stainless steel and brass. I have actually seen some of that equipment still working after 30 plus years in the sun. Not anymore. Even though the manufacturers add UV protection to their plastics, the sun destroys it over time. It won't even be more than a few years before you can easily see the fiberglass shining in the sun. Try rubbing your forearm across that and see why you should make an attempt to prevent it. Of course that's not the biggest reason, the plastic will eventually fail, much sooner than it would if it was in the shade. Pool equipment is not cheap so let's get to work.

You can build a room around the equipment but you may need a permit and I'm sure that this is a pretty expensive option. If you do decide to do this make sure you leave enough space around the equipment and on top of the filter so that you can easily remove the filter top when you need to clean it.

The option I was going to recommend is much less expensive and it can be replaced or removed as needed. A shade tarp with rope on all four corners can be tied to objects around the pool equipment if you have those available. Make sure the shade tarp is high enough for you to be able to walk under it. They are made of a mesh plastic so water will go through them as needed but

Swimming Pool Maintenance Made Easy

they shield a lot of the sun. The other quick option is to simply put a patio umbrella up near the pump and filter to shade it. If you have a lot of wind where you are this might not be a very good suggestion unless you find a good way to anchor the umbrella.

Use your ingenuity and find a way to shade your pool equipment during the summer and you will probably add at least 5 years to its life.

Lifted Concrete Around Pool

When a pool is built the concrete is almost the last thing that is finished before they hand you over the keys, so to speak. Before the concrete is poured there is just dirt around your new pool. What I'm trying to say is that the concrete is just sitting on that dirt so if you plant certain trees that are known to lift concrete too close to the pool it probably will over time. The concrete is usually only 4" thick.

Please do research on all trees that you plan on putting near your pool. Of course you should also think about the amount of debris that each tree will create for your pool as well. There is also the fact that there will be established trees that are already there that may oneway cause damage. You can have a root barrier installed underground if you don't have a choice about the tree and are concerned.

Two types of trees that I know from personal experience damage pool concrete are Palm trees and certain Maple trees (some like Japanese Maple do not). Trees to avoid planting near pools because they develop large surface roots include Norway Maple, Red Maple, Beech, Sweetgum, Eucalyptus, Cottonwood and Weeping Willow.

Trees that I found to be ok around a pool include Hedge Maple, Amur Maple, Japanese Maple, Sweetbay Magnolia, Crabapple, and Japanese Crape Myrtle.

Swimming Pool Maintenance Made Easy

I am certainly not a tree expert and have only learned these few things over the years. You should consult a tree expert or arborist to decide what to do about tree root problems and tree selection.

Settling Concrete

Staying on the topic of trees for a second, some tree roots will pull the moisture out of the soil and make the concrete settle lower over time. Then more roots crowd in to get more moisture and then push the concrete up causing cracks.

Another reason concrete can settle is if the coping above the tile and under the concrete is damaged and water is allowed to erode the soil under the concrete. You can seal this gap above the tile with high quality silicone colored caulking yourself or hire a pool professional to use a more industrial product.

Swimming Pool Maintenance Made Easy

Coping Replacement

The word coping is used to describe the concrete, brick, to other material at the edge of your pool, above the pool tile. There are usually two coping "strips" next to the coping.

The first is just above the tile and below the concrete, brick, or other material as described. This strip is usually sealed well and lasts a long time from the pool builder but sometimes has a plastic edge that starts to pull loose. The plastic can be simply cut off if this happens. Inspect the area behind the plastic strip to make sure water will not be able to get under the concrete causing erosion. If that happens seal the gap with a high quality colored silicone caulk or hire a professional.

The second coping strip is between the coping and the first section of concrete deck. This strip can also be called an expansion joint. The gap is filled with a somewhat flexible product when the pool is built. As a side note, I am seeing new pools without this joint at all (Yay). The product in this joint fails and starts to separate and sink into the crack. It really does start to look bad and most homeowners want to do something about it. Enter the product Deck-O-Seal.

Deck-O-Seal is a two part mix that you can purchase online or at a pool store. It comes in different colors to match your pool and it is relatively easy to install. You have to remove most or all of the current product so that at least 1/2" is available below the level of concrete. You will need to follow the directions on the box of Deck-O-Seal or on their website.

Swimming Pool Maintenance Made Easy

Here is the description of their product from their website:

DESCRIPTION

DECK-O-SEAL two-part, polysulfide-based joint sealant is a premium-grade, pourable, self-leveling sealant. It is a non-staining sealant that cures at an ambient temperature to a firm, flexible, tear-resistant rubber. DECK-O-SEAL is highly resilient and has excellent recovery characteristics after extended periods of compression or elongation. DECK-O-SEAL has outstanding resistance to most chemicals, to all weather conditions, aging, and shrinkage.

USES

DECK-O-SEAL is used for caulking and sealing joints subject to movement to provide a firm, flexible, weather-tight seal. It is ideal for sealing joints on swimming pool decks. It is applicable for both interior and exterior use.

Swimming Pool Maintenance Made Easy

Tile Cleaning and Maintenance

Swimming pool tile will form calcium over time. This is a white build up that is very hard to remove. There are a few things you should know about how to clean the tile and how to keep it clean longer.

Cleaning the tile can be done with certain types of tile cleaning acids and a large pumice stone. Lower the pool water about two inches. The tile acids are usually in a spray bottle and the product will gel up and stay on the tile for several minutes in an attempt to break down the calcium enough for you to scrub it off with the pumice stone. You will only want to spray a 5 foot area at a time. Wait 5 minutes and come back with a wet pumice stone. You will find that this is a very labor intensive process. You will most likely be able to remove a good portion of the calcium but not all. If you really want to get the tile and grout clean you should consider hiring a professional tile cleaner. They will use a glass bead that they blast at the tile inch by inch. The glass bead is recovered so it does not make a huge mess in the pool. The pool water only needs to be lowered about one foot and then refilled. The pool tile will then look like new and so will the grout. Some tile cleaners will add a sealer to the tile to help lengthen the amount of time the tile will stay clean. Professional

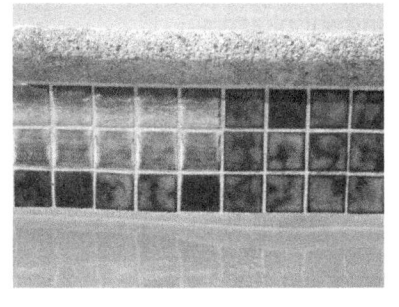

Swimming Pool Maintenance Made Easy

tile cleaning can be very expensive. Currently I have been seeing over $5 per foot.

Either way, after you clean the tile you will want to keep it clean for as long as possible.

The first line of defense is to add a stain and scale preventative (sequestering agent) to the water two times per year. This will stop or at least slow the calcium in the water from precipitating out of the water and forming onto the tile.

The second thing that you can do to slow this process down is to **closely monitor the pH levels in your pool**. A high pH will also cause the calcium to leave the water and form onto the tile. To be honest, a pool that is not closely monitored and balanced will almost always have a lot of calcium build up on the tile. This is because the pH was allowed to raise over time and was never lowered to an acceptable range.

You should also brush your pool tile with a nylon bristle brush once per month to keep dirt, algae, and lotions (scum) from forming to the tile and grout.

Loose or Missing Tile

If you have missing or loose tile around your pool, you will need to make a decision. Are you planning on resurfacing the pool any time soon or are you just trying to preserve the pool the way it is for a while? If you plan to resurface, ask the company you are using to also fix or replace the tile. You can buy missing tile online or at a tile store although they might not match you should

Swimming Pool Maintenance Made Easy

be able to get close. Most of the time it is not very noticeable if the color and size are the same.

Drain the pool a few inches and turn off the pool equipment during the tile repair.

Before you attempt a tile repair check the surface behind the tile called the beam wall. If the beam has holes or con-caved areas, you'll need to shore up the base with hydraulic cement or a plaster mix.

Remove any loose or cracked tile with a grout saw. It's a tool that looks kind of like a screwdriver with a saw blade on top of it.

You can try to re-attach the tile that has fallen off if you still have them. You can do this yourself or hire a tile professional. If you are going to attempt it, the most important thing to remember is good prep work. To prepare the area you are working on you will need to remove as much of the old mortar as possible. You can use a hammer and chisel or grout saw to chip away the mortar so that you will have room for new mortar with the old tile. Make sure you do not damage the beam wall behind the tile. You should also try to remove the mortar from the back of each tile. You can then spread a thin layer of thinset mortar onto the back of the tile (all the way to the edges) and push it on. Thinset mortar will set quickly so you should work quickly to get all of the tile in place. If you are working with a larger area, you can hold the tile in place with thin strips of duct tape. You will need to keep the tape on for 48 hours to ensure a good bond.

After the tile sets you can mix and apply grout using a grout float or flexible spreader. Make sure you use a damp sponge to wipe off

Swimming Pool Maintenance Made Easy

grout that is on the tile itself for a clean finished look. Read the directions on the grout for cure time and then refill the pool.

Swimming Pool Maintenance Made Easy

Removing Rain Water from Pool

Many pools have automatic fill valves in their pool which will keep the water where it needs to be in the summer but very few have a drain line above the normal water level that would keep the water level down during and after a rain storm. This means that you will need to monitor and remove the extra water manually. Why does it matter? Because if the water is allowed to go above the tile and there are any separations in the coping strip, you can cause erosion underneath the concrete deck and even cause dirt to come back into the pool from the same area. The erosion can even cause the concrete deck to settle or crack.

You can also loose pool tile if water gets behind them and then freezes. So how do you remove the water?

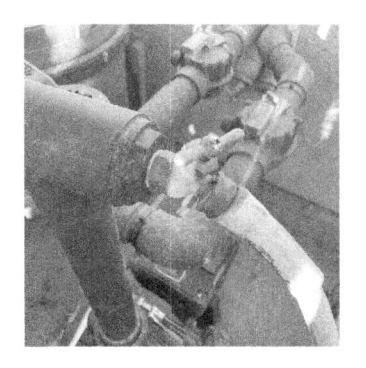

The easiest way to remove the water is to look for a water spigot at the equipment pad in the pool plumbing. It will look like a regular garden hose valve that you can attach a hose to. You can go ahead and attach a hose to that valve and run the hose out to a drain or the sewer cleanup for your house. While the pump is running, open the spigot and water will start pumping out. Set a timer for 30-45 minutes and check on the level of the pool. Reset the time for longer if needed and then shut the valve. Don't forget the timer or you may end up draining out too much water and cause the pump to run dry (without water) which could damage the pump.

The second way to drain water from the pool is to use a submersible pump and hose. You can purchase one of these pumps from a pool store or online. Simply run the hose out to where you want the water to go and put the pump on the first or second step. Plug the pump in and take care so that the end of the plug never gets close to the pool water. I have even tied the cord to something solid and then plugged an extension cord into that, far away from the pool. Set a shorter timer and check the water level. These pumps often pump water quickly so it might not take much time. This depends on the size of the pump and how far away the water is going.

Swimming Pool Maintenance Made Easy

Plaster Problems

Swimming pool plaster can look great for years or it can suffer from poor maintenance and look bad quickly. To be honest, the most common reasons pool plaster doesn't look good have nothing to do with maintenance. Most of the things that happen to a pool surface are a consequence of a poor resurfacing job. Here are some of the things that happen and the reasons why.

Calcium Nodules and their Removal

So you just got your pool resurfaced and a few months or years later you start to see little white spots on the bottom and sides of the pool that look like a formation of some kind. You look a little closer and sure enough, they are hard little calcium like formations, and now you are seeing more all over the pool. What the heck is going on with your new pool plaster?

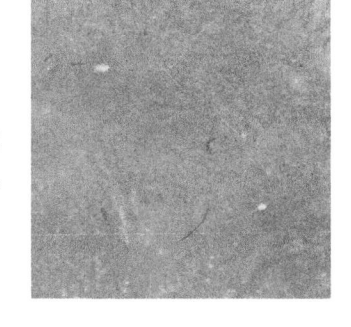

They are called calcium nodules and they form from tiny cracks in the plaster the size of a hair. Chances are, if you find one, you will be able to find many. This is because the thing that caused them wasn't random and isolated, it was most likely the entire plaster job and more specifically the prep work that is causing the issue.

Going back to when you hired the plaster company you may have interviewed a few companies for the job. You may have had one or two of them tell you that they will sandblast or even water

Swimming Pool Maintenance Made Easy

blast all of the old plaster off, all the way down to the gunite. Then you had one or two companies tell you that it is not necessary to do that and that they only sandblast just below the pool tile and they do something different to the surface to prepare it for new plaster (too many variants to list all here). The most common thing they will tell you is that they spray on a bond coat before the new plaster. I'm not saying that all of these cost cutting options are bad because clearly not all pools that were resurfaced in one of these ways end up having problems with calcium nodules. What I am saying is that if the plaster company makes any mistakes with the bond coat and the new plaster does not fully stick to the old surface, you will have problems with calcium nodules.

Basically, calcium will form from the old surface through the new surface and form little sharp calcium mountains all over the pool.

So what now? If too much time has gone by to make the plaster company do anything about the problem themselves, you will end up needing to try to remove them yourself. Luckily you have this book and I just found a working solution on my own pool last year. Yep, my own pool. I went with the cheaper option myself because even I don't know everything about pools, or at least until I learn it (sometimes the hard way). So what's my solution? Believe it or not it was a tool that's been around for years that I wrote off as a gimmick years ago. I don't even remember the product claiming that it can remove calcium nodules specifically. The tool is called a stain

Swimming Pool Maintenance Made Easy

eraser. Calcium nodules are not even a stain. When I first saw the nodules on my pool (plaster was already 7 years old) I started with a pumice stone. The results were not great and it was scratching my Tahoe Blue surface. I called my pool parts supplier and talked to an old friend. I asked what pool pro's were buying for this problem and he said the stain eraser. Really!?! I gave it a try.

The product is like a piece of rubber on the end of a stick with sand inside but you know what? It works. You can see that it has a handle and you can hold that and scrub some of the spots that you can reach by hand but you can really get a lot of leverage when you put it on a good pool pole and scratch away at each spot. Some come off right away with very little effort and some are much harder to remove. Most of the time they are tough to remove is because you can't really get a good angle and push hard enough to scratch it away. Keep working at it and you will be able to remove all of the spots. They will most likely form again but hopefully it will take some time. The was I look at it, I can do this before summer and my family can enjoy the pool and if I have to do it again next year, oh well. I will one day pay to have the pool resurfaced again and this time it will be taken all the way down to the gunite.

Blotching or Modeling Plaster and its Cause

Colored plaster models and if you ask any pool person they will all tell you that it is normal and there is nothing that you can do about it. That is both true and false. Plaster is like concrete and

Swimming Pool Maintenance Made Easy

it has to be mixed before sprayed and troweled on. If you are like most of us, you are adding a color to the plaster instead of having a white pool. The color has to be mixed in as well. It's not as simple as just not mixing the color in all the way but that is definitely part of it. Plaster companies also use concrete accelerants in the mix to speed up the curing time and to deal with different weather situations. Sometimes the accelerants and the color do not mix well and you end up with a spotty, blotchy surface also called modeling or marbleizing. Even a white pool, after it is old enough to see the imperfections, will show modeling too. Proof that it is more the accelerants than the color itself that didn't mix well.

So what can you do to avoid this issue? Don't choose plaster. Plaster is soft and takes almost a year to fully cure. Companies add products to the plaster to try to make a better surface like silicone or accelerants. Ask if the company you want to go with has a product above plaster like quartz crystal or exposed aggregate (pebble) instead. The quartz crystal or similar product is very hard compared to plaster. It does not need accelerants and it will outlast plaster. The color is usually very uniform and if you are thinking about making your pool a slat pool this is the lowest level of a pool surface that is strong enough to not be damaged by the aggressive salt. Pebble surfaces are also strong enough, just more expensive and a little rough on your feet (beautiful though).

Staining, Streaking, or Fading Plaster

Similar the the blotching and modeling issues mentioned above, you can also end up with streaks or faded plaster due to a bad

Swimming Pool Maintenance Made Easy

mix or application of your new pool surface. A bad plaster mix will also stain easier. Please take your time asking a lot of questions to the companies you are thinking of hiring and check the bad reviews online before you sing on the dotted line.

Rust Stains on Plaster

Rust stains can happen on pebble surfaces due to small pieces of metal that were in the mix of rocks that the company sourced for the material. Unfortunately it does happen and it's not really the companies fault. The good thing is it is easy to remove. You can use a pumice stone or stain eraser (mentioned above) to scratch off the rust. Just be careful with pebble surfaces not to be too aggressive and remove a bunch of rock.

Rust can also show up on older plaster surfaces where the plaster is thin and a piece of rebar was not cut short enough and is now protruding into the pool and rusting. Unfortunately this is not as easy to fix. The best answer is to resurface the pool and they will deal with the rebar then. If you would like to get a few more years out of the plaster you can attempt a repair. You will need to drain the pool and grind away the rusted rebar and plaster until no rust shows. You can then etch the surface and go to your local pool store for a plaster repair kit to fill the hole. You can even mix a concrete color into the mix to try and match the color of your plaster. The fix might not last for long but it might buy you a few years. You can also call around to see

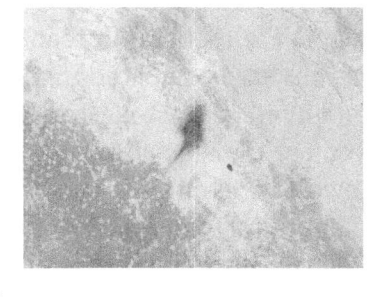

Swimming Pool Maintenance Made Easy

if a pool person around you knows how to do the repair. We used to have one in my area the could even do the repair under water. I don't do this repair so I used him several times. He used to charge about $500 per spot.

Lastly, rust can show up on the pool surface seemingly randomly. The most common reason this happens is from lawn fertilizer. Fertilizer has metals in it and it will definitely cause small rust spots everywhere. Use the stain eraser mentioned above to remove the rust spots. They should be very easy to remove.

Pop Offs and Thin Plaster

Plaster gets thinner and thinner over time and eventually the top layer above the gunite will "Pop Off" leaving behind what looks like a pot hole. These spots are difficult to repair with a plaster repair kit because usually the rest of the plaster around these areas is brittle and will not hold the repair. These spots are mostly cosmetic and is really just a sign that you should be thinking about resurfacing the pool soon.

Tabs in the Skimmer

Here lies a problem for plaster that you can avoid yourself. Please don't put chlorine tabs in the skimmer basket. It ruins a lot of things. One of those things is the plaster at the bottom of the pool by the bottom drain.

The chlorine tabs are very powerful. They are about 90% chlorine compared to liquid chlorine being between 10% and 12.5%. Household bleach is about 4% chlorine. All this chlorine combined with the fact that chlorine tablets are also acidic, you will eventually bleach or etch a round pattern larger than the suction

Swimming Pool Maintenance Made Easy

covers at the bottom of the pool. This is because there is a plumbing line that runs from the skimmer to the bottom suction. When the pump is not running the tabs continue to dissolve and the chlorine seeps down thought the pipe and on to the bottom of the pool. The tabs will also eat away at the pool plumbing making it brittle and anything metal in the equipment will also slowly be ruined.

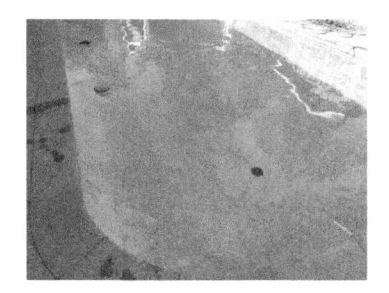

So again, please do not put your chlorine tabs in the skimmer basket. Put them in a floating chlorinator or automatic chlorinator at the pool equipment area as the last piece of equipment with a chemical check valve before it.

Throwing Tabs at the Bottom of the Pool

After reading the last section I'm sure you know that I am going to tell you not to throw chlorine tabs at the bottom of the pool. This is not what the tabs were made for and they will definitely ruin the pool surface. Unfortunately, I have seen this way too many times to not mention it here in my book. Basically it will permanently stain the bottom of your pool. Float the tabs in a chlorine floater and make sure that the lid of the chlorinator locks so that the tabs won't come out when people

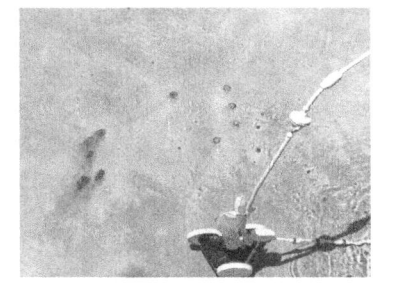

180

are swimming. You might even choose to remove the floating chlorinator while people swim to avoid this issue.

Swimming Pool Maintenance Made Easy

Ducks in My Pool - What you should know

Over the years I have had many customers have the pleasure or annoyance of ducks in their pool, depending on how you look at it. As you probably know, ducks frequently travel in pairs and they are typically looking for a suitable place to lay their eggs and raise their young. If your backyard is inviting enough (lots of bushes and trees) your pool just might be their perfect training waters for 8-12 tiny little ducklings. Cute right? Well...

Ducks do more than just poop in the water. They also fly away during the day and come back several times. The issue is where they go to and what they bring back. Besides the waste that they put into the water they also bring back traces of algae from ponds, rivers, or lakes nearby. There are over 400 kinds of algae that can live in water and some of these algae are not common in a backyard pool. This means that if it takes hold of your water it can be really difficult to kill. I recently had a pool that had a pair of ducks use his yard for their young and he also has a koi pond in his yard. The ducks kept going back and forth as well as the normal, fly away to who knows where, and sure enough we started to get algae. The issue was that I could not kill it. I shocked the pool almost every week and he barricaded the pool so they couldn't get in (they still did). I used two different algaecides 4 times with the shock treatments and we ran the equipment twice as much. The pool never turned green but the algae was all over the walls and after the ducks and ducklings left we hit the pool hard with a very high shock and double dose of

Swimming Pool Maintenance Made Easy

algaecide. We could not kill this algae. His pool surface was at the end of its life anyway and he decided to resurface the pool.

That was last year and guess who is back this year. So he tried doing things that he didn't want to do like running and yelling at them and spraying them with a hose. They would fly away and just come back later. Finally I recommend a solar cover. He bought one right away and it is working. It has only been a few weeks but before they were in his pool daily and they haven't been in since. Time will tell if this works permanently but I would say that it really doesn't have to work for long. As long as they don't see your pool as inviting they should find another one and once they find a private bush to hide their eggs in someone else's yard, they won't want your yard anyway.

Over the years I have seen people buy large floating inflatables, fake ducks, swim noodles, shiny bird deterrents, and more to no avail. I have read that you can add an enzyme to the water and the ducks don't like but I have never tried it so I can't say if it works or not and from what I've read it alters the oil coating on their feathers so it's not something that I would try personally.

A presence of wildlife, including birds, increase the risk of germs and disease such as Crypto, E.coli, Salmonella. Fortunately, most types of bacteria

183

Swimming Pool Maintenance Made Easy

die quickly once they come into contact with the chlorine—this is why it's so important to maintain your pool and its chlorine levels.

I have also seen ducklings end up dead in the skimmer basket because the pool pump is very strong and they get pulled in and can't get back out. If you do have ducklings in your pool it is best to build a ramp so they can get out at the far side of the pool opposite your skimmer if possible.

Swimming Pool Maintenance Made Easy

How Long Should I Run My Pumps?

The rule of thumb is one turnover per day. But what does that mean exactly?

One turnover means all of your pool water is circulated through your filter one time per day. This does not mean that you will actually filter every drop of your pool water. Most likely each day some of the same water enters the pool equipment several times and other water in an inactive corner somewhere does not get filtered at all that day. It only means that you moved your total pool gallonage through your pool filter one time that day.

Remember that new dirt and other contaminates enter the water every day. If you do not accomplish one turnover per day you are likely to build up contaminates that will soon cause algae and other issues. The most common times in the year I see this is in the winter and spring. If you only run the filter half as much as you should you will need to play catch up in the summer to filter out all those particles. If it was too late and algae started in your very fertile water, you may lose half of your short swim season fighting algae that would not have happened if the water started out more "pure" with proper filtration.

Running the pool equipment a couple of hours less than you should during the swim season will cause the same issue as above. More problems with cloudy water and algae will cost you both time and money. You will spend more money on shock and

Swimming Pool Maintenance Made Easy

algaecide than you most likely would have spent on electricity alone.

On the other hand running your pool pump longer than you need to is not needed either. Once the water is clean you only need to maintain that condition. So if you have a large pool party with tons of kids you will want to run the pool extra when everyone is gone to filter out all of the contaminates added to the water by the swimmers. I mentioned it somewhere else in this book but in case you missed it, the average swimmer loses one pint (16 oz.) of sweat per hour! Add that to any dirt, lotion, or sunscreen and you can see why a high use pool needs so much more filtration and chlorination than a low use pool. That's not even thinking about what little kids might do while swimming. Yuck!

Telling you how long to run you filter pump depends on many variables. I would need to know what size the plumbing is, how far the pool equipment is from the pool, what horsepower the current pump is, and what type and size the filter is. Also, Most pools have a variable speed pump so I would also need to know the rpm's that the pump is running at. With all of this considered I could guess for you how many gallons the pool equipment is moving per minute and therefore per hour. **There is a more accurate and easier way for all of this.** If your pool plumbing has a good location for a flow meter to be installed you could add one. The flow meter will tell you exactly how many gallons per minute are moving at any one time. This is also very helpful to show you when there is a problem with the equipment and what the best position for your valves when adjusting for a pool cleaner. If you make a slight adjustment to a valve and the water

Swimming Pool Maintenance Made Easy

flow goes up by 10 gallons per minute that would be great. You would need to make sure the cleaner still has enough power to work properly but if it does you will move more water per hour and therefore need to run the pump less per day saving you money on your energy bill.

If you do install a flow meter you will be able to precisely know how many hours to run your pump per day. Let's say your flow meter says you are moving 65 gallons per minute. Multiply that by 60 (for 60 minutes in an hour) to see that you are moving 3,900 gallons per hour. If your pool is 18,000 gallons you will need to run your pool 4.6 hours per day.

The flow meter does have certain requirements to work correctly. It needs to be installed after the pool filter and before any cleaner lines or other water feature. You also need about 12" of straight pipe to put the flow meter. Many times there is not an ideal place to install a flow meter. They do sell flow meters that install on pipes that are vertical instead of horizontal if that helps. The reason you do not want to install the flow meter before the filter is because small debris will enter the meter and clog it. Follow the instructions from the flow meter for proper installation. I use a flow meter made by "Blue White".

There is a new flow meter that is also a check valve called a FloVIS by H2Flow Controls. Check valves are used in pools frequently and you can buy just the insides of this valve and insert them into the housing of your old check valve. Then as the valve opens when water flows through it, you can see the Gallons Per Minute (GPM). These flowmeters are very accurate and can detect flow down to 5 gpm. This is especially helpful when running a variable speed pump at a very low speed. If you don't have a check valve in your pool pluming you can still have one of these installed by a pool professional.

The last and easiest way to see the GPM is to look on the display of your Sta Rite or Pentair Variable Speed and Flow Pump (VSF). Only this one model (VSF) will show you currently but I am sure more variable speed pumps will do this in the future. On the Sta Rite and Pentair VSF pumps, simply push the right arrow until is shows you the GPM. It will also show you the RPM's, Watts it is pulling, and pressure (PSI) in the system. Just keep hitting the right arrow while the pump is running and it will cycle through these readings.

Booster Pumps

Also called a pool cleaner pump, booster pumps only need to run long enough to have your pool cleaner keep your pool clean, usually between 2-3 hours per day. Booster pumps are not self priming pumps and do not pull water. Because of this they need to run during the time that your main pump runs to be supplied water. I usually start the booster pump timer about an hour after the main filter pump turns on to make sure all air is out of the plumbing lines and it will be safe to run the pump. As I said, 2 or 3 hours later you can set it to shut off. The main pump will continue to run for its remaining run time. If you have a variable speed pump you should make sure that the RPM's of the variable speed pump are high enough to supply enough water to the booster pump so damage does not occur. Most variable speed pumps need to be set to at least 1200 RPMs to be sure. For me this is not usually an issue because I usually set my variable speed

Swimming Pool Maintenance Made Easy

pumps to run between 1,800 - 2,100 RPMs during the pool run cycle.

Swimming Pool Maintenance Made Easy

Main Drain Covers

The main drain is the round drain at the bottom of the pool usually in the deepest spot. It is not actually a drain but a suction line instead. There are two ways that this line can be plumbed.

The first is the most common. Usually the pipe that comes from the main drain goes under the pool and then up to the bottom of the skimmer. If you remove the basket and regulator from the skimmer and see two holes at the bottom then your pool is plumbed this way. What that means is that the only way that the drain at the bottom ever has any suction is if the regulator partially or fully shuts off the suction from the top of the pool which forces the water to be pulled from the bottom of the pool. The regulator serves two functions. There is a float inside the regulator that will engage if there is an obstruction like too many leaves in the basket or a very low water level in the pool. For both situations the pool pump will not run dry and the pump will get its water from the bottom of the pool instead of the top.

The second way the bottom drain can be plumbed is directly to the pool equipment with a valve to determine where the water is pulled from. You would have control of how much water is pulled from the bottom or top of the pool. With this type of installation you will see another cover about 2' under the skimmer on the wall of your pool. This is a separate line plumbed to the skimmer in case the pool is too low or there are too many leaves. There are also older pools that do not have this safety feature at all. If

Swimming Pool Maintenance Made Easy

the pool water is too low and the main drain is not on, the pool pump will run dry. That might ruin the pool motor in just a few hours (or less).

If you are re-surfacing your pool I highly recommend a channel drain instead of the new round covers because of how high the round covers are. The pool cleaners will get stuck on the tall covers many times. The channel drains are nice looking and are flat to the pool surface.

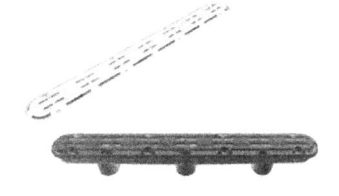

If you are missing your main drain cover you must replace it with a new cover that meets today's safety codes. It is very possible for people to become entrapped in the open line by their hair or body. People have lost their lives this way and that is the reason for the new covers and more strict codes.

Swimming Pool Maintenance Made Easy

Safety Signs, Equipment, and Rules

Swimming pools can be fun and exciting, and for many places they are almost necessary to escape the heat. Swimming pools can be a great tool to keep your kids close during their summer break, but don't forget this important thought. Pool safety is a very important topic. We have all heard our parents yell out "No running around the pool". I am sure now that most of us are parents we say the same things. The truth of the matter is that there are certain precautions that you can take to make your swimming pool a safer place.

Signage – I believe we should all have at least one sign for our residential pools posted on a wall or fence that we use when others come over to use our pools. It is a tool to convey our intent to have a safe situation at all times. The sign should serve as a reminder to your own kids every time they use the pool that they too need to follow the rules. I am passionate about this because way too many accidents happen every year from running around the pool, jumping into a pool incorrectly, hitting heads or chins on pool walls from goofing off, and so many more. I think that if you tell everyone who uses the pool that these rules need to be followed or they cannot use the pool, you will have a much safer pool.

Pole with Hook – Along with the normal metal pole that you most likely have for your cleaning equipment, it is a smart idea to have

Swimming Pool Maintenance Made Easy

a safety pole with the attached safety hook on the end. The pole is 16' long with no extender in the middle. This is important because the extender is likely to slip when pulling someone to safety. You need a long and solid pole mounted near the pool so it can be grabbed at a moment's notice. The hook on the end is shaped to easily pull someone in need out of the pool quickly and safely. This is a small investment that could save someone's life.

Swimming Lessons - It is important that anyone allowed to swim already knows how to swim. This alone does not guarantee their safety but it is an important first step. Anyone who does not know how to swim needs to have constant adult supervision inside the swimming pool (not outside). Never assume that a life jacket or floaties will protect your child.

Supervision - Direct adult supervision is a must at any pool event. I can't urge this enough because just being in the same area as the pool is often not enough. Unfortunately most drownings are not heard even when there were adults in the area. Someone needs to watch children to ensure their safety and enforce the pool rules. I have heard too many stories over the years not to stress this like I am. Sorry.

Swim with a Buddy - When children are old enough with plenty of swimming experience you might let them swim without a parent or adult sitting there the entire time. I urge you to demand that any child, no matter what their age, always swim with a buddy. Even teenagers can get hurt messing around and

Swimming Pool Maintenance Made Easy

end up drowning if there is no one around to help out. Always swim with a buddy!

Suction Covers - Never let the bottom drain go uncovered. The section above labeled "Main Drain Covers" goes over the details regarding how these drains work and the types of compliant covers available. The important part here is to realize that there really is an entrapment issue if the suction drain "Main Drain" is not covered with the appropriate cover. They are even more dangerous if they are left uncovered entirely. Adults and children alike can become trapped by their bodies or hair and possibly drown because a $25 cover was not installed.

Pool Fence - Having a pool fence around your pool just might be the best decision you can make. You will still have easy access to your pool through a secure self-closing and self-latching gate. I believe the peace of mind is worth the price you might pay to install a safety fence around your pool.

Safety Covers - Another alternative to a pool fence is a safety cover. This type of cover fastens to the pool deck directly and would be difficult or impossible for a child to remove. It uses springs and a latching system to attach to the deck. Safety covers are very strong. Most safety covers have a 200 lb. per square inch

Swimming Pool Maintenance Made Easy

strength. I once saw an advertisement for a safety cover with a baby elephant and a family standing in the middle of a pool on top of a cover. It is important to realize that most of these covers do allow water to flow through it so if a child was to walk on the cover and the water level below the cover was not low enough there would be enough water on top of the cover to drown. This type of cover is usually used to winterize or shut the pool down for the off season.

Pool Alarms - There are pool alarms that can be installed on the gate of the pool as well as the style that sit on the water and wait for water movement to sound off. Use one of these tools as a backup to a locking gate or door alarms on every door exiting to the pool.

Door Alarms - If you are having a pool installed you will need to buy door alarms for every door that exits to the pool area. This alarm is installed at the top of the door and a button needs to be pushed before the door is opened to prevent the alarm from sounding. Any child opening a door will not be able to reach the button and the alarm will sound. A pool gate is still the best option for safety. It is better to get used to using door alarms rather than doing what most do, which is to remove the alarm after they pass inspection.

Water Vest or Life Jacket - A life jacket can be used in a swimming pool as a small extra to help protect your child. A jacket should never be used to

Swimming Pool Maintenance Made Easy

protect your child while they swim. Any child could end up upside down with the jacket on without direct supervision. Instead, use the jacket on your child when they are just hanging out by the pool. Just in case they fall in when you are not looking. It may give you enough time to safely get to your child.

CPR Certified - It would always be nice if someone who is CPR certified was available to sit by the pool whenever someone was using it. Unfortunately that will probably not happen but you may consider taking a CPR class yourself to for added protection from disaster.

Important! If a child is ever lost, look in the pool or spa first. It may make the difference between life and death.

Swimming Pool Maintenance Made Easy

Pool Lights – Differences

There are a few different types of pool lights that you might have installed in your pool. The most common type is a standard incandescent flood light inside a waterproof light assembly about 2' below the top of the pool. These lights are usually white only. If you prefer a color lens, you can buy a blue or red plastic cover that snaps onto the standard light.

The second most common styles are color lights. There are actually a few types of color lights. Halogen lights are just like the regular light mentioned above except the light can change colors. Most color lights include 5 or 7 colors. Most will change slowly between the colors and offer a flashing "party mode" as well. Halogen lights are brighter than the other color light which is an LED light. The LED light also has the "party mode" and rotates between the colors. The biggest differences between these two lights is that the LED light uses much less energy and has a very long life. The average LED light bulb has a life expectancy of over 11,000 hours. The halogen light might last 2,000 hours.

The last light style is fiber optic. Fiber optic has to be installed when your pool is built. They also change color but there is no quick flashing between the colors (party mode). This style light has a light box outside of the pool where there is a halogen light bulb with a color wheel that slowly spins. The downside to this light is the light box has a fan that runs to keep the halogen bulb cool and that fan can be a little loud. You also have the short life

Swimming Pool Maintenance Made Easy

of the halogen bulb. The bulb is very easy to change though. When this light system is used it is not uncommon for there to be fiber string under spillways and several small round light sources in the pool and spa to create a well-lit pool.

Changing out a light

I believe that you should hire a professional to change out a burnt out light for a few reasons. The pool light is a dangerous thing if there is a leak. The light should be checked when it is apart to ensure the condition of the light is good enough to re-install. New safety codes are always changing and it helps to have a professional look at your light and make sure it is up to code and grounded. They will also be able to check the GFCI that the light goes through to ensure protection against a faulty or leaking pool light.

If you do want to change out the light bulb you will be able to find this information online so even though I believe you should hire a professional I will cover the basics here.

The standard light as well as the LED and halogen styles all come apart the same way. LED lights should never need to be taken apart. Follow these steps to change out your light bulb.

- Always insure the power is off before removing the light assembly. Shut off any breakers that might send power to the light.

- Remove the light assembly by

Swimming Pool Maintenance Made Easy

unscrewing the Philips screw at the top of the light. The light will then tilt forward and then unhook from the bottom of the light niche.

- There is enough cord for the light to be pulled up and out of the pool water. It should rest safely on the pool deck above the light niche.

- Identify the clamp behind the face of the light. There are a few different styles of clamps that you might have. Most are a single stainless steel ring that separates in one location with a bolt and nut. The other is a series of small triangular pieces with a screw in each of them all the way around the circle. Each screw would be loosened or the clamp removed and the assembly will pull apart.

- The light lens (glass) will have a rubber gasket around it. It is important to replace this gasket as well as the bulb inside the light.

- Check to see if there is any water inside the light. If there is you should pay a professional to install a new light. It is not worth putting things back together that may not seal and could cause injury or death.

- Check to see if you see any rust inside or outside the light assembly. If there is you should have the assembly replaced.

- Take the light bulb and gasket with lens to a pool store to have them help you pick out the correct replacements.

Swimming Pool Maintenance Made Easy

- Before you put things back together make sure you notice that the lens is usually directional. It is usually labeled "top". Make sure that marking aligns with the Philips screw at the top of the ring.

- Install the new light bulb. Do not turn the light on until it is safely back in the pool. Most of these lights get very hot and are water cooled (around the light assembly).

- Take care to put the gasket on the lens in the right direction and look around the light ring to ensure it is even before tightening the clamp.

- Tighten the clamp evenly. If you are unsure that the light went back together correctly I strongly recommend that you hire a professional to finish installing the light.

- Lower the light into the water and coil the cord around the cone shaped back of the light assembly.

- Hook the bottom of the light into the light niche.

- Re-attach the Philips screw at the top of the light to secure the light.

- There should be no one in the pool when it is tested.

- Look for water inside the light before turning the breakers back on and testing the light. You can usually see a water line that was not there before behind the lens if there is water in the light.

Swimming Pool Maintenance Made Easy

- Turn the breakers back on and flip the switch. If the light trips the breaker or GFCI turn the breakers back off and call a professional. If the light works correctly, leave it in for a few hours and re-check for water in the light. If everything looks good you have accomplished the replacement of your pool light bulb. Congratulations. Check your light for water or damage from time to time. Never, I really do mean Never, operate a pool light without a GFCI.

Swimming Pool Maintenance Made Easy

Safety Covers

As mentioned in the safety section above, safety covers are a good option if you do not have a fence around your pool or are looking for a way to keep all of the debris out of your pool during the winter.

Pool safety covers are very strong. Most have a tensile strength of several hundred pounds per square inch (check with the manufacturer of your cover for specific ratings). You should not try to walk on the cover but if you needed to you certainly could. They are a great investment because they give you peace of mind if you ever have children in or around your house. The covers fasten to the concrete deck of your pool with a spring and loop assembly so it is unlikely that a child could remove part of the cover or find a way to get under the cover when properly attached.

Safety covers are sold as mesh and solid. Mesh will allow water to go through the cover and also some sunlight while the solid covers prevent both. Mesh covers do not need water removed off of them at any time while a solid one might build up a pool of water that needs to be drained off. Mesh covers allow some sunlight to get through so algae is still possible and a solid cover basically prevents the possibility of algae. Either cover is safe and a good option to help with easier fall and winter maintenance.

Solar Covers

Pool solar covers are popular because they work well. They will raise the pool water temperature by an average of 10-15 degrees. They will also extend your swimming season by about one month on both sides of the normal season. Solar covers will also slow down water evaporation. There are a few downsides to a solar cover as well.

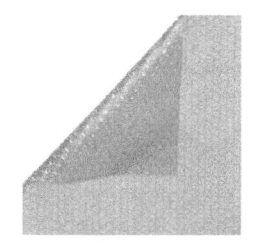

The covers are difficult to remove all in one piece if you cannot use a solar reel. If it is too bulky or heavy you should consider cutting the cover in half or thirds through the middle so you can remove smaller sections instead.

When the cover is off you will be folding and storing the cover somewhere by the pool. It is important to protect the cover when folded by keeping it in the shade or covering with a tarp. The folded cover might melt onto itself if not protected.

Pool solar covers are a safety risk. Take great care to never allow kids to play around a pool that is covered. If a child or adult falls into the pool when the cover is on it is very difficult to get out of the pool because the cover will not hold the weight and you will sink into the pool with the cover around you.

Keeping the cover on for too long will cause a very high water temperature and algae is almost guaranteed. Only use the cover to reach the desired temperature and then remove the cover for a while.

Swimming Pool Maintenance Made Easy

Solar covers are purchased by length and width in the shape of a rectangle. Measure your pools longest and widest points and go with a cover that will fit. You do not have to cover 100% of your pool if you do not want to. As long as you cover about 80% of the surface you will get great results. Unfold the cover and lay it across the water bubble side down. The cover will need to rest on the water for a few hours so that the folds go away. After the cover relaxes, use a pair of scissors and cut the cover to the shape of the pool. It doesn't have to be perfect, just try to cut it so the cover floats on the water all the way around. You don't want the cover to go up the tile or especially up onto the deck. These covers are meant to float on the pool water directly. Remember, bubble side down.

Solar Panels on Your House

Many homes already have solar water panels on the roofs of our home. Many more wish they did, and for good reason. The solar covers mentioned above work very well but they are cumbersome and need to be cleaned often to continue to look nice. With solar on your roof you will achieve the warm water and the extended swim season that you desire without the headache. There are a few things that you need to know to be able to properly maintain your solar system.

The system will be turned off for the winter (we will discuss this soon) so you will need to turn it back on. The best time to do this

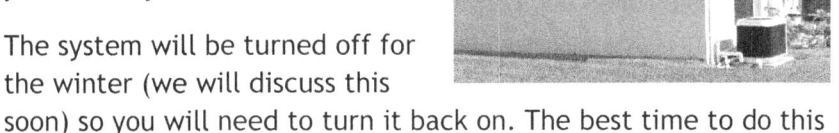

Swimming Pool Maintenance Made Easy

is in spring right before the summer season. The rule of thumb is that you will want a forecast of both warm days and warm nights for the next week or more. If the nights are still cold you will lose any temperature that you might gain during the day each night. It is a good idea to have someone show you how to turn the system on and off the first year but here is the breakdown.

- Make sure the pool equipment is off.

- There are usually two shut off valves located in the pool plumbing that goes up the wall to the solar. They will be shut off and you will need to turn them both on to allow water to flow.

- You are likely to have drain valves located in the plumbing either here next to those shut off valves or on the roof at the corner of the lowest solar panel. It is possible to have three or more drain valves but two is the most common. These valves look just like a garden hose valve. You will need to shut all of the valves you find. If you miss one you will see it when the system is turned on because water will flow out of it. This will not hurt the system; just turn it off once you locate it.

- There is one more valve that turns two directions in the shape of a "T". If you have automatic controls for your solar you will not need to do anything with this valve because when you turn the system on the valve will turn automatically. If you have a manual system you will need to turn the valve the opposite way to send the pool water up to the solar.

Swimming Pool Maintenance Made Easy

- If you have automatic solar controls you will find a switch on the panel that says "Test", "Auto", and "Off". Move this switch from "Off" to "Auto".

- Move the dial for your desired temperature to the highest temperature that you want the water to reach before shutting off. If you set this too high and we are in the middle of a hot summer you might end up with water that is too hot and suffer some of the warm water conditions mentioned below.

- Turn the pump on and watch the pressure on top of the filter. The pressure will be higher than it was when the solar was off but you should not hear any loud pump noises or see extremely high pressure on this gauge. If you do experience any of these things you need to turn the pump back off and check the positions of all of the valves. If you are unsure if something is correct you should call a professional. Running the pump with the valves in the wrong position can cause damage to the pool equipment, injury, or even death from the high pressure that will build up.

- Walk around your house and look for any water coming from the solar panels. Leaks are common when the solar is turned back on for the first time. Most of the time a solar company will be able to fix the leaks easily at a low cost. This is just regular maintenance.

- If everything looks good and the water flow is strong in your pool then you have successfully turned the solar system on. You should see warmer water over the next week. Make sure you change the run times of the filter and cleaner pumps to run during the hottest parts of the day to get the best results. The hottest hours of the day are from 12:00 pm -6:00 pm.

To turn the solar off after the swim season is complete you will reverse this process. The most important part is that you make sure you open all of the drain valves to allow all of the water to exit the panels. Leave the drain valves open all winter in case there is any water left in the panels. This will give that small amount of water room to expand during freezing conditions without causing any damage. Make sure you also shut the two shut-off valves going to the solar and turn the "T" valve the other way to bi-pass the solar. If you have automatic controls for your solar make sure you slide the switch to "Off".

There are many solar companies that offer a service to turn on and off the solar every year for you. They will usually go up on the roof each year and tighten all fittings and fix any small leaks for a very reasonable price. It may be worth the peace of mind. Call several companies for their prices.

Warm Water Conditions

Water can be warmed by a gas heater, electric heater, heat pump, solar cover, or solar on the roof. No matter which way you heat your pool you should take care not to heat the water too high. As mentioned above, water that is too warm will likely have

Swimming Pool Maintenance Made Easy

algae problems throughout the summer season. The only preventative against this is to increase the run times for your filter pump and use a preventative algaecide (algaecide 60) often. You can add a maintenance dose every week. You will most likely need to keep the chlorine levels at 5ppm the entire time your water temperature is over 80 degrees.

Swimming Pool Maintenance Made Easy

Summary

Taking care of your swimming pool can be an easy task. You just need to perform weekly tasks and keep track of your testing results to ensure you are not missing a week of maintenance and letting your pool start to have problems. I highly recommend using the log on the website to hold you accountable. I think you will find over time it is nice to be able to look back at those results to learn more about your pool. It also removes any question of when something was done like the last time you cleaned the filter or tested the conditioner and calcium levels. Keep the log on a clipboard by your test kit and use it every week. I use a log for every pool that I maintain, including my pool at home.

Always look for algae in the spring, summer, and fall and use a 60% algaecide as soon as you see it. Catching it early makes all the difference and don't forget to brush and shock with the algaecide. Maintain the chlorine between 3-5 ppm and the pH at 7.4 as much as possible. Don't let your conditioner level get above 80 ppm. I try to keep the pools I take care of at 60 ppm. Keep the filters clean and run the pump the right number of hours per day depending on the time of year to ensure a clean and healthy swimming pool. Buy a flow meter and install it in the PVC to show you how many gallons of water are really moving per minute or use the one on your variable speed pump if it has one. This will allow you to calculate how many gallons are moving per hour. Then you divide that number into your pools total gallonage and you will know how many hours to run your pump in the

Swimming Pool Maintenance Made Easy

summer. Flow meters are available at most pool stores. Products like this and other high quality cleaning equipment not available at most stores will soon be available at www.mypoolmadeeasy.com

That's the summed up version.

I hope you found the information in this book helpful. **Please feel free to email me any questions not addressed in this book. I will try and answer all questions as soon as possible and add the new topic to the website.** My main goal for writing this book was to make owning a swimming pool a little less intimidating. You can always hire a pool service to do the work for you but not all pool services are created equal. You will at least have more information on your side to ensure they do their job correctly and not overcharge you for things you do not need. Good luck with your pool maintenance! I hope you have the most beautiful and easy to maintain pool on your block! **If you enjoyed this book please do me a giant favor and rate it on Amazon!** The reviews are hard to come by and I appreciate them very much. Thank you!

Website: www.mypoolmadeeasy.com Weekly pool maintenance log is available at this website.

Swimming Pool Maintenance Made Easy

Glossary with Lots of Extra Information:

Chlorine: Used as a sanitizer for pool water. To sanitize means to kill all living organisms. There are four common chlorine products used in swimming pools; 1. Liquid Chlorine 2. Tablet Chlorine 3. Granular Chlorine 4. Shock.

Free Chlorine: Free chlorine is the chlorine that is still available to sanitize the water after the rest of the chlorine in the water has combined itself with other contaminates. See combined chlorine below.

Combined Chlorine: When chlorine combines with contaminates in the water such as sweat, oils, lotions, algae, dirt, or viruses, it stays combined until oxidized out. Combined chlorine produces the characteristic "chlorine odor" (chloramines) that most think is from too much chlorine in the water. To oxidize the water you will need to shock the pool. This is most common in high use pools and spas. See shocking the pool for more info.

Shocking the Pool: You can shock the pool to rid the pool of contaminates, kill algae, and oxidize the water. It is also called "breakpoint chlorination". To accomplish this you must first test the "free chlorine" and "total chlorine" levels. Subtract the "free chlorine" from the "total chlorine" to get the "combined chlorine" level. Then multiply the "combined chlorine" level by 10. Add enough chlorine to

Swimming Pool Maintenance Made Easy

raise your chlorine level by this amount. Example: If your "combined chlorine" was 1 ppm, you will need to raise your chlorine level 10 ppm higher than it is now to remove the "combined chlorine". You can also add a non-chlorine shock at the rate of 1 lb. per 10,000 gallons and then raise chlorine levels normally. Shocking the pool water is most often needed after a large pool party or heavy rain because of the amount of material now in the water. Non-chlorine shock will not kill algae.

pH: A measure of how basic or acidic the pool water is. Too low causes eye and skin irritation as well as damage to the pool and pool equipment. Low pH can also cause stains on the pool surface from iron and copper that was broken down. Too high causes scale formation on pool surfaces and possibly pool filters. Ideal range for all swimming pools is 7.4 – 7.6. Acceptable range is 7.2 – 7.8.

Alkalinity: A buffer for the pH. If this reading is high, the pH is difficult to move. If this level is low, the pH bounces around too easily. Ideal range for a plaster pool is 80 – 120 ppm. Ideal range for a fiberglass or vinyl pool is 100 – 140 ppm.

Conditioner: Also called stabilizer, this product is added to the pool to protect the chlorine from the harmful rays of the sun. Without enough of this in the water the sunlight will remove the chlorine too quickly. Ideal range is 60-80 ppm. Acceptable range goes up to 100 ppm. Please remember, if

Swimming Pool Maintenance Made Easy

your conditioner level is high, it will take a lot more chlorine to keep your pool water sanitary and free from algae. Most people would not want to swim in that much chlorine. I recommend that you keep the conditioner levels close to 60 ppm.

Calcium Hardness: **A measurement of how hard the water is. Pool water that is too soft will pull the calcium that it wants out of the pool plaster or metal components of the pool equipment or plumbing over time. Too high levels of calcium can cause scale build up on pool walls, tile, and filter systems. That happens most often when the pH and the calcium levels are high together. It is also thought that too high of a calcium level interferes with the working of chlorine.**

Phosphates: **All water has phosphates introduced to it every day. They come from different things that enter the pool including swimmers and their clothes. Keeping a low level of phosphates will reduce or eliminate the potential for algae in your pool. It is difficult to keep this level low all the time and should be checked if algae is a continual problem in your pool. If the level is high it will be worth lowering and establishing a ritual of adding small amounts of phosphate remover to keep the level low. Especially if your pool is prone to algae. Don't forget to clean your filter about a week after you add the phosphate remover. Please read the section in the book about phosphate removers before you**

Swimming Pool Maintenance Made Easy

decide to use them including about my decision to not use them.

Sequestering Agent: A sequestering agent is a liquid you can add to the pool to prevent stains and scale build-up. It keeps heavy metals and minerals in solution and does not let them precipitate out onto the walls or tile. If you use a lot of copper algaecide you should also use a sequestering agent often. If you have had stains on your pool and have removed them you should also use this product. You can add a sequestering agent as much as once per month or as little as once per year. The average would be two times per year to prevent most stains. One time before fall because of the leaves that might sit at the bottom of the pool, and in spring because of the potential chemicals you might add during the spring and summer season.

Total Dissolved Solids: A measure of all the chemicals or other dissolved material that were ever added to this pool water. Some of those particles build up in the water and start to interfere with the working of chlorine as a sanitizer. Most pools go through enough dilution through evaporation and splash-out to keep this number small. If this level gets over 1500 ppm the pool should be drained part way and refilled to dilute it down. Please note that if this happens the conditioner and calcium levels will need to be re-balanced.

Swimming Pool Maintenance Made Easy

Pool Filter: The type of filter media that is responsible for removing small particles from the pool water. These particles cause poor water conditions that lower the effectiveness and longevity of pool chlorine. Small particles are also considered food for algae. The smaller the particle you can remove, the easier your pool will be to maintain.

Cartridge Filter: A fibrous material used to trap large particles from the water. This type of pool filter needs to have the water pass through many times to pick up a smaller and smaller particle. The end result is a very small particle removed from the pool water and a filter that is very easy to clean. Just a garden hose is usually needed. The average 300 square foot cartridge filter will hold up to 15 lbs. of dirt or material. They will remove particles down to 9-11 microns. We can only see down to 30 microns and a human hair is about 60 microns thick. This is the most common type of pool filter.

Diatomaceous Earth (D.E.) Filter: D.E. is a powder that coats a grid assembly inside this type of filter. From a technical point of view this filter is superior to a cartridge because they remove smaller particles. All the way down to 1-5 microns in size. They will remove these particles with only one or two pass-through. The downside is they need cleaning a lot more often or they will suffer damage in the form of crushed or torn grids inside. Also, the dry powder is dangerous if inhaled. The microscopic hooks seen with this

Swimming Pool Maintenance Made Easy

powder clings to your lungs and won't come out. People working with this product unsafely and often are prone to lung cancer over time.

Sand Filter: A very easy filter to clean. Just a valve is used and the water is reversed through the filter to wash out the dirt. The filter is not often chosen because it only traps particles down to 30 microns in size and we can see down to that size. This sometimes means you will have slightly hazy water with more chance for algae.

Pool Pump (Also called the filter pump): This piece of equipment is responsible for moving the water to and from the pool and pushing that water through the filter. The right size (Horse Power) pump running the right number of hours per day will accomplish one turnover per day as required.

Here are the types of pool filter pumps.

Single Speed Pump: They used to be the most common pump but have since mostly been replaced by variable speed pumps because of the cost savings. Single speed pumps run in one speed and should be sized correctly for the given situation when the pump and filter are installed. Valves are sometimes used to control different features in the pool or spa with only one pump.

Two Speed Pump: This was the first pump developed to try and save money running the pump in a lower speed for the bulk of the day and then high speed for a couple of hours

Swimming Pool Maintenance Made Easy

per day so pool cleaners and other equipment can run. The big issue with this pump is if you calculate how many gallons the pump moved and the energy used, the low speed does not always save you money compared to a single speed or especially variable speed pump, running the correct number of hours per day.

Variable Speed Pump: This pump has completely changed the way we think about pool pumps and what they can do. They save you hundreds of dollars per year in energy costs and they are very quiet. The other big advantage is that one pump can be used for several different objectives. For instance, if the solar is on the pump will run at a different speed than it would if the spa jets are on. They match up to a controller to make all this possible. It is also not a copper winding motor, instead, it is a permanent magnetic motor similar to those used in electric cars.

Booster Pump: This pump is used for automatic pressure side pool cleaners. They take a small amount of water from the filter pump and put that water under a lot of pressure making the pool cleaner move. These pool cleaners are more powerful that others and the rest of the water the filter pump moves is available for general circulation or other water features.

Swimming Pool Maintenance Made Easy

Pool Heaters: The piece of equipment is responsible for heating the pool water. Here are the different types.

Gas Heater: This is the most common pool or spa heater used in the past and present. It is the most cost effective way to heat water for an attached spa. Most heaters are only used in the spring or fall to help extend the pool season. Solar heaters on the roof are better to extend the season because once you own the system it is free to run versus the gas you have to continue to buy to use this heater.

Electric Heater: They can be used to heat a pool or spa where gas is not available. The usage costs are significantly higher than gas and therefore this heater is not very common.

Solar Heat: The most efficient way to warm the pool before and after the pool season. Solar will extend and make a more comfortable summer as well. They are not practical for heating an attached spa.

Heat Pump: The heat pump is plumbed into the pool equipment like a regular heater and just electricity is used. They are much more efficient than an electric heater but cannot accomplish the same rise in temperature. It is basically an air conditioner running in reverse. They are still not as efficient as a gas heater or solar on the roof.

Timers: Pool timers are used for each of the pool equipment pumps. The first is for the filter pump, and the second is for

Swimming Pool Maintenance Made Easy

the booster pump (for pool cleaner). Then there could be optional timers beyond that that might control a waterfall pump, pool light, or other auxiliary feature. Pool timers are meant to turn something on and back off every day so you don't have to do it manually.

Automatic Controls: There are several brands of automatic controls but features are similar in all. Most have a panel in the house on the wall or a handheld wireless display that lets you turn pool equipment on and off manually. Of course you can also get a wireless transmitter and receiver that plugs into your modem in the house and now be able to control your pool from your phone even when you are thousands of miles away. This does come in very handy when you know that your spa takes 30 minutes to heat up and you are 30 minutes from home right now. Lol

The system also holds many automatic programs for any water feature, pump, pool light, outdoor lights, or even sound systems outside. Most can also turn the pool or spa heater on and automatically turn the pool valves to spa mode with the push of a button. There are also temperature readouts for both the water and air temperature outside.

Digital Timer: More like the standard mechanical timer, most digital timers only turn a few things on or off when programed. There is no panel inside the house and no temperature readouts.

Swimming Pool Maintenance Made Easy

Mechanical Timer: The standard timer. Only controls one piece of equipment per timer. Simply turns one pump on and off each day. Usually a yellow round wheel with small "trippers" on the dial. One tripper says on, and one says off. You can loosen the screw on the tripper and slide it to a different time to adjust when the pump goes on or off. To adjust the time on this timer you pull the dial towards you and rotate until the silver arrow points to the correct time of day.

Pool Cleaners: You can use different tools to clean the top and bottom of the swimming pool. The most common type is the automatic pool cleaner. There are many brands. They fit into two different styles. Suction side and pressure side pool cleaners. The distinction is made because of the side of the pool equipment they are part of.

Suction Side Automatic Cleaners: This style pool cleaner attaches to the suction side of the pool equipment through the skimmer or dedicated suction line at the side of the pool. All debris they pick up heads toward the pool equipment and get trapped in an inline leaf trap or the pump basket directly. The small debris that gets through the baskets end up in the pool filter. This type of cleaner has a few disadvantages compared to a pressure side pool cleaner. The pool filter gets dirty a lot faster than one using a pressure side filter and the size of debris is limited to small

Swimming Pool Maintenance Made Easy

leaves because of the small opening at the bottom of these cleaners.

Pressure Side Automatic Cleaners: This is the most popular style of pool cleaner. The Polaris is the cleaner that is used most often. These pool cleaners are plumbed to the pressure side of the pool equipment. They work with the water returning to the pool. They create suction at the pool cleaner itself and force debris into the pool cleaner bag by way of venturi system. That means that water jets at the bottom of the pool cleaner point up into the cleaners bag and the pool water and debris gets pulled up into the bag. Some of these cleaners use a small booster pump to make them more powerful and some just use the main filter pump and a valve to determine how much water they receive. This style cleaner traps over 70% of the debris before it makes its way to the pool filter. That means you will not need to clean the filter as often. The standard bag on these cleaners will even hold sand and silt.

Electronic Pool Cleaners: This style cleaner comes with an electrical cord that you plug into an electrical outlet for the cleaner to run. They are popular for pools that were not designed for a suction or pressure pool cleaner and would therefore have to be cleaned with manual pool nets otherwise. They work well but should only be run for about two hours at a time or the cord will begin to get tangled. Most have a bag or filter system inside where the debris is

Swimming Pool Maintenance Made Easy

trapped. They are easy to clean. The disadvantage is that you have to put them in the pool and remove them when you want to clean the pool. Other automatic cleaners run every day without you thinking about it.

Pool Surfaces: Most swimming pools are made with a concrete called gunite reinforced with metal rebar. This is not a suitable pool surface because it does not hold water and can be very rough. Several surfaces have been developed over the years. They usually offer a smooth water tight finish that looks great. There are differences to the way you maintain each surface and what you should expect from each.

Plaster: The most common type of pool surface. This surface is very smooth and can have color added to give you a desired look. The most common color added is "Tahoe Blue" which is a dark grey surface. White is also very common. The blue sky reflects with the white surface giving the look of blue water. Plaster requires a pH of 7.2-7.8 to be maintained at all times. It also requires a calcium hardness level of 200-400 ppm. The chlorine should be maintained between 1-5 ppm. The alkalinity needs to be between 80-120 ppm. If the proper chemical levels are maintained this pool surface will last for 15-20 years. Minor staining starts showing up on white surfaces after about 10 years. A sequestering agent can be used twice a year to slow down this process. The surface will eventually deteriorate and even flake off in areas causing small pot holes where the plaster was too thin. The pool would need to be sandblasted and resurfaced to resolve these issues. Improper chemical balance will speed up this process.

Exposed Aggregate (Pebble Tech): Similar to plaster with small rocks added to the mix. The Plaster that holds it together is usually grey and not really noticeable because of the number of rocks added. The size of rock is usually smaller than a quarter of an inch. Some are even smaller than that. They are smooth to the touch. Some swimmers say after a while using the pool their feet hurt a little. This pool surface is very resistant to chemicals and deterioration. Some call this surface "bullet proof". This surface does work very well when used as a salt pool. Most people choose this surface because they love the way it looks. You can choose the colors of the rocks as well.

Fiberglass: Most fiberglass pools are a shell that is lowered into the ground and the installer finishes the work and fills in dirt up to the walls. A concrete deck is still used and the pool looks very nice. Some of the problems with this type of pool are that the original owner gets to choose the extra features for the pool. They may not see the importance of a main drain at the bottom of the pool or a dedicated pool cleaner plumbing line so you may not have them. If these items are missing or if there are only one or two return lines, you may have a difficult time maintaining

Swimming Pool Maintenance Made Easy

this pool. The fiberglass surface does last a long time but it is possible to ruin the "gel coating" covering the fiberglass with poor chemical maintenance. The pH on fiberglass pools is always trending down so it is important to raise the pH as needed.

It is also possible to have a normal pool that needs to be resurfaced and you can choose to have the pool fiberglassed instead of plastered. The same is true about the chemical balance mentioned above.

All fiberglass is very slick and sometimes people slip in this style pool.

Note: It has been my experience that the "gel coating" wears away on the steps and swim outs after people use those areas for years. Then the fiberglass is exposed slightly and will be prone to staining.

Vinyl Liner: There are many in-ground vinyl liner swimming pools that have been installed. Similar to the fiberglass pool above, the surface is slick and the pH trends down requiring pH increaser many times per year. There is no "gel coat" to worry about but the liner itself needs extra care. The vinyl is thin enough to have holes poked through it with hard plastic toys, dogs feet, pool cleaning equipment, or anything else sharp or hard. The liner should last about 15 years if you take care of it. If holes are created they can be patched by a vinyl repair person. You should not use tablet or liquid chlorine with a vinyl pool. Instead use granular chlorine only.

Pool Skimmer: The skimmer has a lid covering it in the concrete deck of the pool. It is located next to the pool. Inside you will find a basket that catches leaves. Under the basket is a plastic device called a regulator. It is sort of mushroom shaped and the flat larger side goes down when you put it back. If you look at the bottom of the regulator you will see a plastic tear drop shaped adjuster and a hole in the middle. If you cover this hole with the adjuster and put the regulator back in, the pump will not pull the water from the top of the pool, instead it will pull the water from the main drain at the bottom of the pool. Most people leave this adjuster covering about half of the hole. The regulator also is a safety device. There is a float inside the unit that will automatically start pulling from the bottom of the pool only if the water level is too low. You should never count on this device to perform this function because it can fail. It is better to keep a close eye on the water level to make sure it never goes below the halfway point of the pool tile. The skimmer also has a small door in the opening to the pool. This door is called a "weir". The weir hinges from the bottom and swings back and forth. When the pump is on the weir gets pulled towards the skimmer allowing debris to enter the skimmer and get stop at the basket below. When the pump stops the weir floats back upright creating a door so the debris cannot go back into the pool. Replacement

Swimming Pool Maintenance Made Easy

weirs are available at any pool store if it is missing or broken.

Note: You may have more than one skimmer.

Main Drain: The main drain is located at the deepest part of the pool in the middle. It has a plastic cover over it with small holes preventing people or object from getting stuck at the bottom of the pool from the suction of the pump. It is not actually a drain at all. It is a suction line that is controlled by the regulator in the skimmer or a valve at the pool equipment. There have been many changes to the covers over the years to prevent hair or body entrapment from happening. Commercial swimming pools have even more restrictions when it comes to these covers and even the pump that pulls from them. This is because the pumps used in a commercial pool is usually much larger and more powerful than a residential pool pump. They are now equipped with a vacuum release system that will shut off the pump if there is an entrapment issue. This style pump is sold for residential swimming pools if you feel more comfortable having one. It is important to make sure that the cover meets the current standards and is not broken or missing at any time.

Note: I highly recommend a channel drain if you are resurfacing your pool. They are rectangular with curved corners and completely flat and smooth to the pool surface. Often they are sold to match the color of the new surface so you hardly see them. The other covers that meet the new code requirements are raised up enough to sometimes interfere with the workings of the pool cleaner.

Return Lines: The return lines are simply the small plumbing lines that are coming back from the pool equipment with filtered pool water to be returned to the pool. There are usually at least 5 return lines for the average pool. They are located on the side of the pool wall or at the bottom of the pool with small covers over them. If they are in the walls of the pool they will often have a plastic eyeball fitting attached. This eyeball is adjustable. It is standard that all the eyeballs are turned to create a whirlpool effect in the pool. This keeps the dirt and debris moving and available for the skimmer and main drain to trap them. If they are at the bottom of the pool they usually point to each other until the debris ends up at the bottom of the deep end of the pool for easy removal.

Pop up Jets (Caretaker System): This is a variation of the in floor return lines mentioned above. The clean water from the pool equipment first goes to an automatic valve called a "module" that rotates between one or two jets at the bottom of the pool. This gives each jet more pressure and the debris has a better chance ending up in a trap at the bottom of the pool or just at the main drain.

Valves: Pool valves are used to change the direction of water to or from the pool pump for a different desired effect. Most

Swimming Pool Maintenance Made Easy

valves have a handle you turn manually, but some valves turn by themselves with a valve actuator hooked up to automatic controls. When you push the button for spa, the valves turn to operate the spa. Below is a better description of each kind of valve.

3 Way Valves: The 3 way valve is the most common valve you will see as part of the pool equipment plumbing. There are 3 sides to this valve. The first is the "inlet" side. That is the side where the water comes into the valve. The other two sides are where the water can go. There is a handle on the top of the valve that you can rotate either direction to slowly shut off the water to one side or the other depending on your desired effect. The most common 3 way valve brand is "Jandy". The Jandy valve has the word off on one side of the handle. If the word off is all the way to one side of the valve then no water will go that direction.

Shut-off Valves: These valves are most often used to stop water when something is shut down manually. Solar being shut off and drained for the winter will use shut off valves to make sure no new water enters the solar. If your pool equipment is lower than the water level of your pool, you will need shutoff valves allowing you to stop the water when you need to clean the pump basket or filter. Never forget to open the valves before the pumps are turned back on. They are similar to the 3 way valves but with only 2 sides.

Swimming Pool Maintenance Made Easy

Check Valves: These valves only allow water to go one direction through the valve. There is no handle on this valve. There is a flapper or spring that opens when the water is flowing and when the water stops it keeps it where it is. Check valves are often used with solar and attached spas that are higher than the pool water level. If this check valve fails the water from the raised spa will drain back into the pool when the pump stays off for several hours.

Baskets: Used to trap leafs and other debris for easy removal. They are used in a few different areas of your pool. Below is a better description of where they are and when they need to be cleaned.

Skimmer Baskets: The skimmer basket is in the concrete deck of your pool near the pool water. There is a lid that covers the hole you use to get the basket out. A rock or weight may be required to keep in the basket to stop it from floating when the pump is off. This basket needs to be emptied at least once per week.

Pump Baskets: The pump basket is inside the filter pump. There is usually a clear lid that unscrews to remove the basket. This basket only receives debris from the bottom of the pool or suction side pool cleaner with no "in line leaf trap" installed. Any debris that gets past the skimmer basket will also end up in this basket. Pump baskets typically only need to be emptied every other week. You should check it every week by looking through the clear lid at the amount of

Swimming Pool Maintenance Made Easy

debris in the basket. If the water flow ever slows down this is the first place you should check.

In Line Trap Basket: If you have a suction side pool cleaner you should have an in line leaf trap. Inside that trap is a plastic basket or cloth bag used to trap leaves and other debris before they make their way to the pump basket. Most of these in line traps have a ring you need to unscrew by hand to get to the basket. The trap is in between two sections of hose close to the wall of the pool.

Pool Lights: There are a few different types of pool and spa lights used today. They are all designed to be under water (water tight). If you ever notice water or a water line inside one of these lights you should turn the breaker off for the lights and have it replaced.

Standard Light: The most common pool and spa light still today. This light only comes with a white light bulb but you can put a color lens over the glass on the outside of the light if you wish. They are usually 500 watts and are very bright. The bulbs will last about 2,000 hours most of the time. Most pool owners only use the light infrequently so the cost to run the light really does not matter. If you run this light a lot it will cost you quite a bit more than a LED light and will not last you very long.

LED Light: This is the most efficient pool light available. They are about 86% more efficient that a standard or halogen light of the same brightness. They also last for an unbelievable amount of time. They are rated at 11.4 years of continuous use. LED lights are available in just white or a 5 or 7 color light that will change between colors or stay at a desired color. They even have a party mode that quickly changes between the 5 or 7 colors. It goes great with music. The only disadvantage is that they are not as bright as a standard bulb or halogen. They are about 30% less bright.

Halogen Light: These lights came out before the LED color light. They also come in white and color. The bulbs inside are very bright and last about the same as the standard light. They are not very energy efficient either. They do rotate between colors and most have a party mode. The advantage is how bright they are. They are about 30% brighter than the LED version.

Fiber Optic Light: Fiber optic lights cannot be converted to any other light style. You only see small holes with covers in the pool. Behind the cover a fiber optic cord is run to a metal box with a halogen light and a color wheel inside. There is also a fan that can seem loud to keep the bulb cool. There is no party mode with this kind of light. You need to turn this light on at the metal control box. If you have an automatic control system it may be hooked up to the fiber optic light and you will not need to turn it on and off at the light box.

Swimming Pool Maintenance Made Easy

Chlorinators: Tablet chlorine dissolves very slowly. They need to be in a place where water will move past them to be introduced to the pool. Because tabs are 90% chlorine (very strong), they need to be contained to be safe for the swimmers and the pool. If the tabs fall out into the pool they will sit on the bottom and cause a stain that does not go away easily.

In-Line Chlorinator: Some pools have an in-line chlorinator at the pool equipment that holds the tablet chlorine. The in-line chlorinator is plumbed into the PVC piping itself. There is a dial setting from 1-5 indicating the speed you wish the tabs to dissolve. Bigger pools or ones with large bather demands will need the highest setting. You can put 2-5 tabs in the chlorinator per week. Water is sent through the unit to help dissolve the tabs faster.

Off Line Chlorinator: The off-line chlorinator is the same as the in-line chlorinator except it is not installed in the pools plumbing. It sits on the ground next to the pool equipment and has two small tubes going to the PVC piping instead. Water still goes through the chlorinator the same way.

Floating Chlorinator: The floating chlorinator is the most common place to put the chlorine tabs. The floater just sits in the pool and floats around. There is an adjustment at the bottom of the floater to increase or decrease the amount of chlorine released. The lid locks so the tabs do not accidentally come out. Always replace the floater if the lid no longer locks. One of the problems with the floating chlorinator is that it might sit on a step or swim-out depending on their height. There are different lengths floating chlorinators available for this reason. If they sit on a step they will cause a stain.

Made in the USA
Coppell, TX
20 May 2022